Ecclesiology in Reformed Perspective

THE RUTHERFORD CENTRE FOR REFORMED THEOLOGY
ECCLESIOLOGY SERIES

SERIES EDITORS

A. T. B. McGowan and John McClean

The Rutherford Centre for Reformed Theology (RCRT), based in Scotland, has established "The Ecclesiology Project" to enable some serious reconsideration of the Reformed doctrine of the church. The project is carried out in partnership with the Theological Commission of the World Reformed Fellowship (WRF).

Ecclesiology in Reformed Perspective

Billy Kristanto

PICKWICK *Publications* · Eugene, Oregon

ECCLESIOLOGY IN REFORMED PERSPECTIVE

The RCRT Ecclesiology Project

Pickwick Publications
An Imprint of Wipf and Stock Publishers
199 W. 8th Ave., Suite 3
Eugene, OR 97401

www.wipfandstock.com

PAPERBACK ISBN: 978-1-6667-1015-1
HARDCOVER ISBN: 978-1-6667-1016-8
EBOOK ISBN: 978-1-6667-1017-5

Cataloguing-in-Publication data:

Names: Kristantos, Billy, author.
Title: Ecclesiology in Reformed perspective / Billy Kristanto.
Description: Eugene, OR: Pickwick Publications, 2022. | The RCRT Ecclesiology Project. | Includes bibliographical references and index.
Identifiers: ISBN 978-1-6667-1015-1 (paperback). | ISBN 978-1-6667-1016-8 (hardcover). | ISBN 978-1-6667-1017-5 (ebook).
Subjects: LSCH: Reformed church—Doctrines. | Church.
Classification: BV600.3 K75 2022 (print). | BV600.3 (ebook).

To Rev. Stephen Tong,
from whom I learn the beauty of Reformed theology

Considering the challenges we face in these most uncertain and troubling times, this careful and refreshing study, highlighting the divine origin of the church is more than welcome. When the body of Christ feeds abundantly on the written and incarnate word of God it is better able to fulfil its calling and to bear witness to the light of the world. As it seeks to further the Kingdom, it is crucial for the church to proclaim with audacity and love the truth, the beauty and the relevance of the whole counsel of the Lord. I heartily recommend the reading of Billy Kristanto's thought provoking and edifying book.

—**Pierre Berthoud**, *Professor emeritus, Faculté Jean Calvin*

This study of the church gets to the point economically and effectively. The author has the knack of focussing on essentials while at the same time incorporating and usefully referencing an impressive range of authors, both ancient and modern, from different church traditions. Taking as starting point the church as the creation of the Word, Billy Kristanto constantly reminds us that while having a human form, the church is the expression of God's choice and act. Founded by Christ, the Chalcedonian model provides a way of understanding its calling as witness to Christ in mission—both in institution and events.

—**Paul Wells**, *Editor in chief* Unio cum Christo

This is a wonderfully clear and concise ecclesiology with an emphasis on the Reformations and the Reformed traditions. The book offers rich insights into the offices, the ministries and the attributes of the church (unity, holiness, catholicity, apostolicity). It illuminates the importance of the sacraments and the relation between the church and the reign of God. It is ideal for the study in church communities, in schools, seminaries and universities.

—**Michael Welker**, *Senior Professor,*
    University of Heidelberg in Germany

Kristanto combines in this ecclesiology a breadth and international orientation that is rarely seen: voices from both sides of Atlantic are brought together in a dialogue that helps to understand the church as a provisional community called by the living Christ. Drawing from the rich well of reformed theology substantial reflection and contextual awareness go together in this intelligent study.

—**Cornelis van der Kooi**, *Professor Emeritus*
    Vrije Universiteit Amsterdam

Contents

Series Foreword

THE RUTHERFORD CENTRE FOR Reformed Theology (RCRT), based in Scotland, has established "The Ecclesiology Project" to enable some serious reconsideration of the Reformed doctrine of the church. The project is carried out in partnership with the Theological Commission of the World Reformed Fellowship (WRF), which is also currently engaged in a study on ecclesiology.

On many of the doctrines of the Christian faith, there is broad agreement within the community of Reformed Christians. If we were considering the Trinity, the Person and Work of Christ, the doctrines which make up our understanding of salvation (effectual calling, regeneration, justification, adoption, repentance etc.) then the disagreements among us would be minor. When it comes to the doctrine of the church, however, there is no such agreement. We believe that there is a great need today for clarity in our understanding of the church, not least its nature and purpose.

In the seventeenth century, the ministers and theologians who wrote the *Westminster Confession of Faith* had a very "high" view of the church. They affirmed that the church is "the kingdom of the Lord Jesus Christ, the house and family of God, out of which there is no ordinary possibility of salvation." In the twenty-first century, many people have a very "low" view of the church, seeming to regard the church almost as an optional extra. Within the community of churches that trace their origins back to the sixteenth-century Reformation, both of these views are represented and also everything in between. How then should we formulate a doctrine of the church that is true to our roots and that is also fit for purpose in the twenty-first century?

In this series there will be several monographs on the subject, two of them being on aspects of the unity of the church, which we believe to be a vital topic in our divided church situation. Given our Reformed beliefs that the church should be confessional and that its worship should con-form to the "Regulative Principle" (the idea that we may only do in worship what God commands), we are including in the series the WRF Statement of Faith (a new Reformed confessional statement) and a new edition of the *Reformed Book of Common Order*. Also included will be the papers from the Edinburgh Dogmatics Conference, which took place at the beginning of June 2020 and was focussed on the subject of ecclesiology. We hope in due course to add other volumes to the series.

We hope that you will both enjoy and benefit from this series.

A.T.B. McGowan, editor
Director of the Rutherford Centre for Reformed Theology (www.rcrt.scot)
John McClean, deputy editor
Vice Principal of Christ College, Sydney (https://christcollege.edu.au)

Preface

THIS ECCLESIOLOGICAL STUDY ARGUES that Reformed ecclesiology cannot be separated from Reformed Christology. The Christological foundation of Reformed doctrine of the church will be examined, since Reformed theology portrays the important ecclesiological topics in the light of its Christological thoughts. This book offers potentials for the future of the church with her pastoral concern. The book will serve as a challenge to the erroneous paths of ecclesiocentrism on one hand and church-forgetfulness on the other. Even though the chapters of the book deal with classical topics in ecclesiology, it will try to analyse and answer contemporary challenges faced by the church.

Discussing the material also in dialogue with other theological traditions, my book distinctively presents a Reformed perspective. With special emphasis on Calvin, it will also cover broader Reformed perspective. Besides systematically covering the classical topics in ecclesiology, the book will also approach the topics in biblical and historical perspective.

The most important contribution of this book is perhaps that it encourages us to view the church not from a modern survivalist struggle, but from the perspective of the theology of creation, the doctrine of Trinity, Christology, pneumatology, anthropology, and soteriology as important criteria of truth for ecclesiology. Just as Christ is not without his church, the church is not without her Head. However, this is not a systematic treatment in the sense of an examination of the whole developed in terms of one principle, which is Christology. Rather, we are concerned to expound the Holy Scripture realistically and to engage with the contemporary church in her concrete existence. The study will weave together insights from biblical, historical, confessional, philosophical, and contemporary studies in a fruitful way.

I presented parts of chapters in this book in my church ministries in Germany and Indonesia. I thank my congregations in Indonesia and Germany for their patient support in the process of writing. I am grateful for the supportive understanding of my wife and children who have sacrificed their family time. Gratitude are due to Dr. Andrew T. B. McGowan and Dr. John McClean as the editors of the Rutherford Centre for Reformed Theology Ecclesiology Series, as well as all colleagues in the Theology Commission of the World Reformed Fellowship for their encouraging and critical comments in the gradual making of this book. Great thanks to the team of the publisher, Wipf and Stock, who made the entire publication process possible.

Billy Kristanto
Singapore, August 2021

Abbreviations

BECNT	The Baker Exegetical Commentary on the New Testament
CCEL	Christian Classics Ethereal Library
CD	Karl Barth, *Church Dogmatics*
CR	Corpus reformatorum
CTJ	*Calvin Theological Journal*
ERT	*Evangelical Review of Theology*
FC	The Fathers of the Church
HC	Heidelberg Catechism
JTH	*Journal of Theoretical Humanities*
KuD	*Kerygma und Dogma*
LW	Luther's Works
MTJ	*Mid-America Journal of Theology*
NPNF I	Nicene and Post-Nicene Christian Fathers, Series 1
NPNF II	Nicene and Post-Nicene Christian Fathers, Series 2
NTOA	Novum Testamentum et Orbis Antiquus
QD	Quaestiones disputatae
TRE	*Theologische Realenzyklopädie*
WA	Weimarer Ausgabe of Martin Luther's works
WBC	World Biblical Commentary
WCF	Westminster Confession of Faith

WRF   World Reformed Fellowship

WUNT   Wissenchaftliche Untersuchungen zum Neuen Testament

Introduction

THIS BOOK IS A concise ecclesiology written from a Reformed perspective. The book will present systematically the classical topics in ecclesiology and engage various dialogue partners not only from Reformed, but also from other traditions as well. Beside the systematic approach, this ecclesiology shall also include biblical theology, historical theology (Reformed traditions in general and Calvin in particular), and some philosophical discussions. The presence of some contemporary philosophers, though their thoughts are not directly related to ecclesiology, shall enrich and contextualize the historical issues in our contemporary ecclesiological situation.

Our postmodern theology is very cautious against an idealized and universalized model of the church.[1] The failure of modern idealism has been acknowledged since a long time ago. We share this concern in this book yet at the same time, we believe that to engage with concrete sinfulness of the church, we need the descriptions of what the church is supposed to be. The concreteness of the church needs not to exclude the questions on the nature, the attributes, and the ministries of the church. Thus, this book will cover both the "ontological" and the "practical" thinking about the church.

The uniqueness of the book is perhaps that it offers contextual insights into the classical ecclesiological topics. It shall encourage us to view the church not as a static being with all her ideal characteristics but as a being in becoming. The church is the beloved bride of Christ to be, who is still being sanctified by her bridegroom until she will be presented without spot, wrinkle, and blemish (cf. Eph 5:26–27).

---

1. See, for instance, Healy's critique on what he calls "blueprint ecclesiologies." Cf. Healy, *Church, World and the Christian Life*, 25–51.

1

An orthodox Reformed ecclesiology should not be discussed separately from the other theological loci. Here, we can affirm Lossky's Christological application to the church, though only to a certain extent. It is wrong to exclusively apply Christology while ignoring anthropology and soteriology in relation to ecclesiology. The book shall serve as a warning against the erroneous paths of ecclesiocentrism on the one hand and church-forgetfulness on the other.

On positive notes, the book seeks to formulate the broad spectrum of meanings of the church, the search for her relevance, and the false adoration of the church. The first chapter begins with the church's divine origin: she is a creature of the divine Word. The Chalcedonian model, along with anthropology and soteriology, which can provide a way of understanding the double aspect of the church's visibility and invisibility is the content of the second chapter. The third chapter postulates that the Scripture primarily describes the church non-ontologically as it is evident from the rich use of metaphors for the church. The following Chapters 4–7 open up aspects of the nature of the church from the government and officers of the church, the ministries, the sacraments, and the four historical attributes of the church. Though these chapters deal with the church's nature, that is, with the questions of what makes a church a church or when a church might cease to be a church, we do not lose sight of the concrete sinfulness of the church. Finally, the last chapter surveys different alternatives on the relation between the church, the kingdom of God, and the public life while offering an ecclesiological position at the end.

We should mention a few remarks on the limitations of this book. As the title indicates, this book is written from a Reformed perspective. Though written with an emphasis on the Reformed traditions, interactions with other theological traditions as dialogue partners should not be excluded. By the adjective "Reformed" we mean the inclusion of the most important Reformed confessions and catechisms along with a particular emphasis on the thought of John Calvin. While humbly acknowledging that there is alternative ecclesiological traditions, we try to offer a meaningful synthetic reflection from a Reformed perspective. This book might also be regarded as "evangelical" in that it invites its readers to participate in the life of the church as a creature of the gospel of Christ.

The presentation of the book is intended for students in theological seminaries and universities, but also for church pastors who want to rethink the church in our contemporary context without losing confessional and historical perspectives.

1

Creatura Verbi Divini

WE BEGIN WITH THE divine origin of the church. A reformational ecclesiology should begin with the triune God who speaks through his Word in the power of his Spirit. After drawing from Luther, this chapter will present a biblical theology of the church from creation-theological perspective. As the creature of the Word, the church should be committed to proclaim the whole counsel of God. Though the true gospel remains the same, it needs to be addressed context-sensitively from time to time. We use Levinas as an example of contemporary philosopher, whose question can be addressed by the message of the gospel. The same principle applies to Nehamas, Hume, and Scruton, yet this time in the context of contemporary notions of beauty. This chapter will then be concluded with Bernard's mystical experience on the beauty of the Word.

1.1. Luther on the Church

The church is the creature of the Word of God according to Luther. It means she is totally dependent on the faithful and abundant teachings of the Word of God. She will lose her attraction, her uniqueness, and her beauty apart from the Word of God. Luther famously wrote:

> For since the church owes its birth to the Word, is nourished, aided and strengthened by it, it is obvious that it cannot be without the Word. If it is without the Word it ceases to be a church.[1]

1. Luther, LW 40, 37.

3

In its light, the Word brings the church to true knowledge of herself.

The seven churches in Asia are addressed by the Word of Christ through John (cf. Rev 2–3). The fallenness of the churches can only be revived by the power of the Word. The Word brings the church to the knowledge of her weakness and her strength, whether it is the abandonment of her first love, false teachings, sexual immorality, her incomplete works, her lukewarmness, or her faithfulness in the midst of tribulation and her patient endurance. The divine knowledge upon the churches is one of the elements that belong to the structural pattern of all the seven messages. The tradition of biblical prophets behind the notion of this divine omniscience can be found in Jer 48:30; Hos 5:3; Amos 5:12; 1 Cor 14:24–25; Luke 7:39; John 4:19.[2] Every church is called to know herself truly in the light of the Word of Christ. "Without knowledge of God there is no knowledge of self," wrote Calvin.[3] Coherently, without knowledge of the Word there is no knowledge of the church.

Believing in God's creative power means giving up the self-creative power of the church. The church is a movement started by Christ himself through his creative Word. Luther was very much aware of the temptation to preserve the church by his own power. Though as a Christian he was called to do his part in preserving the burning candle of God, in his treatise *Against the Antinomians* Luther wrote:

> For after all, we are not the ones who can preserve the church, nor were our forefathers able to do so. Nor will our successors have this power. No, it was, is, and will be he who says, "I am with you always, to the close of the age."[4]

Committing the church to God and his power is not a sign of antinomianism.[5] On the contrary, it humbly realizes the danger of self-creative power of church ministers.

The Holy Scripture draws a contrast between a true theology of creation and self-made human creation. In the story of creation, we read that God brought all living creatures to Adam to give each of them a name (cf. Gen 2:19). Even Eve was given a name by Adam (cf. Gen 3:20). On the

---

2. Cf. Boring, *Revelation*, 89.

3. Calvin, *Institutes*, I.1.2.

4. Luther, LW 47, 118.

5. Antinomianism is a heretical teaching that rejects the continuity of the moral law in the life of the believer. The WCF maintains that the moral law "doth for ever bind all, as well justified persons as others, to the obedience thereof." WCF XIX.5.

contrary, in the story of the self-made tower of Babel, humans wanted to "make a name" for themselves (cf. Gen 11:4). Thus, here identity is acquired by self-creative power. On the danger of this desperate lust to be remembered, Henry comments, "Rather than die and leave no memorandum behind them, they would leave this monument of their pride, and ambition, and folly."[6] The church should not struggle for her own identity for her identity is given by God instead of acquired by self-achievement (cf. Matt 3:17; 4:3). What is needed for the church is the power to overcome the Devil's temptation by resisting the tempter with the abundance of the Word of God.

Not only does the church need to resist the tempter, but also to preach the abundance of the Word to the world. Our pluralistic society needs multifaceted pictures of Christ.[7] The church needs to preach not only the Johannine or Pauline Christ, but also the Markan, Matthean, or Lukan Christ. When Zwingli started his expository preaching with the Gospel of Matthew at the Grossmünster in Zurich, he was certainly driven by the unsatisfactory reductive preaching of his time. It took him six years to preach through all of the New Testament writings. Similarly, during his ministry in Geneva, Calvin preached thousands of sermons on almost every book of Holy Scripture.[8] Without abundant preaching of the Holy Scripture, the church will be left in a destitute and miserable condition. A healthy church should offer the best spiritual delicacies for the society.

The church should be faithful to the preaching of the gospel. As "the creature of the Gospel," the church is "incomparably less than the Gospel."[9] This is not to say that Luther had a low ecclesiological view. He could continue Cyprian's famous dictum "Salus extra ecclesiam non est" (outside the church there is no salvation) in his *Large Catechism*: "For where Christ is not preached, there is no Holy Spirit to create, call, and gather the Christian church, and *outside it no one* can come to the Lord Christ."[10] For Luther, salvation means no other than coming to Christ. When there is no gospel of Christ preached and heard, the local visible church has lost her most

6. Henry, *Commentary on the Whole Bible*, 32.

7. I have written elsewhere on the need to explore the aesthetic mode of the Word of God against its reductive view. Cf. Kristanto, "Bible and our Postmodern World," 162.

8. For a detail description, see Parker, *Calvin's Preaching*, 153ff.

9. "Ecclesia . . . creatura est Euangelii, incomparabiliter minor ipso." Luther, *Resolutiones Lutherianae*, WA 2, 430, 6–7.

10. Book of Concord, 416; italics mine.

valuable treasure. "The true treasure of the church is the most holy gospel of the glory and grace of God," wrote Luther.[11]

1.2. Same Word—Different Contexts

The true gospel remains the same, yet, its opponents vary from time to time. Jesus is always the answer; yet, the church needs to listen very carefully to the questions posed by each context. When Jesus declared, "Come to me, all who labor and are heavy laden, and I will give you rest" (Matt 11:28), his invitation was addressed to the law-burdened, upon whom the Scribes and the Pharisees have laid an unbearable burden (cf. Matt 23:4).[12] Now, we have a new form of legalism, i.e. neo-legalism forcing many churches to be politically correct, to accept the label homophobia because of their view of traditional Christian marriage, to be more pluralistic while giving up their orthodox belief, to be involved in neo-Marxist social agendas, etc. In the context of societal neo-legalism, humans are expected to perform successfully to attain acceptance and love. In religious context, believers are demanded to show and prove impressive religious achievements and activities to obtain God's favor. The list can go on. Jesus's message remains the same: "the truth will set you free" (John 8:32). The gospel has a liberating force for the law-burdened. The church needs to context-sensitively address the forms of this neo-legalism.

The message of the gospel can also be seen as the ultimate answer for the most focussed and detailed philosophical questions. For instance, the love of Christ is the final goal for the search of Levinas' "infinite responsibility" for the Other, in which the authority of the face of the Other is felt.[13] Levinas saw Cain's failure in his responsibility for his brother as a violation of the face.[14] Cain failed to rule over his sinful desire for mastery by the

---

11. Luther, *The 95 Theses*, no. 62.

12. Cf. Hare, *Matthew*, 128.

13. Levinas, *Entre Nous*, 74.

14. Commenting on Cain and Abel, Levinas wrote, "The face, it is inviolable; these eyes absolutely without protection, the most naked part of the human body, offer, nevertheless, an absolute resistance to possession, an absolute resistance in which the temptation of murder is inscribed: the temptation of an absolute negation. The Other is the sole being that one can be tempted to kill. This temptation of murder and this impossibility of murder constitute the very vision of the face. To see a face is already to hear: "Thou shalt not kill." Levinas, *Difficile liberté*, 22.

assertion of the sovereignty of his freedom,[15] because his *face* had fallen (cf. Gen 4:5–7). His failure to encounter Abel face-to-face was a result of not-being-forgiven or not-being-accepted by God.[16] The offering refers to God's forgiveness or God's acceptance in Christ but Cain did not receive this forgiveness so that his face fell. In other words, only through God's forgiveness in Christ do we have the power to rule over our sinful desire to harm our neighbor. Christ is the acceptance of God who empowers humans to encounter face-to-face, to love their neighbors. Being forgiven precedes loving our neighbors.

When the gospel is purely preached, the church continues to exist, according to Calvin, for in the doctrine of the gospel, the true religion prevails.[17] The preaching of the gospel should be handed down from generation to generation, so that the church continues to witness the true religion. "It is by the preaching of the grace of God alone that the church is kept from perishing."[18] God sustains the existence of his church from generation to generation; it is the responsibility of Christian parents to teach the doctrine of grace to their children.

Quoting the Puritan's understanding of the gospel, Packer has reminded us that we must opt for the comprehensiveness of the gospel instead of "high-speed evangelism" which harps merely "on a few great truths—guilt, and atonement, and forgiveness—set virtually in a theological vacuum."[19] Thus, for John Owen, gospel promises are "The . . . gracious dispensations, and, discoveries of God's good-will and love, to, sinners through Christ in a covenant of grace; wherein, . . . he engageth himself to be their God, to give his Son unto them and for them, and his Holy Spirit to abide with them, . . . and to bring them to an enjoyment of him."[20] Such comprehensive sum of the gospel can only be preached faithfully in the church as a long-term venture. It requires rich understanding of the attributes of God, the doctrine of the Trinity and its applications, the doctrine of humanity and sin, the salvation history, the whole gracious work of God in Christ, the church as community of believers, the hope of the church. Evangelical churches

15. Cf. Levinas, *Totality and Infinity*, 84.

16. Cf. Wenham, *Genesis 1–15*, 106.

17. Cf. Calvin, *Comm.* Ps 122:8, in *Calvin's Commentaries: Psalms* (electronic ed.).

18. Calvin, *Comm.* Ps 22:31.

19. Packer, "The Puritan View of Preaching the Gospel," in *Puritan Papers*, vol. 1, ed. Lloyd-Jones, 256, 263.

20. Owen, *Works*, vol. 11, 227.

should be critical of reductive notions of the gospel. Such reductive views tend to become a cliché.

Underestimating the inexhaustibility of the Scripture is one of the greatest sins of churches. To quote Owen, church ministers "need not fear farther useful interpretations of the Scripture, or the several parts of it, than as yet have been attained unto by the endeavors of others; for the stores of truth laid up in it are inexhaustible."[21] The way to that inexhaustible treasure is through humility and diligence, which for Owen, is the same thing as giving up oneself unto the Spirit's conduct. Owen's pneumatological grounding for his homiletics reflects Pauline *theologia crucis* (cf. 1 Cor 2:4). Practical-theologically, the vastness of Scripture is accessible through piety: "I suppose, therefore, this may be fixed on as a *common principle of Christianity*, namely, that constant and fervent prayer for the divine assistance of the Holy Spirit is such an indispensable means for the attaining the knowledge of the mind of God in the Scripture."[22] Not only does prayer safeguard the church from poor understanding of Scripture, it also protects the church from the final pervasiveness of harmful error of every fundamental truth. Truth is inexhaustible; on the contrary, error or ignorance is limited and reductive.

God has given the church his inexhaustible Word. The Reformed churches always regard the Word as a means of grace. In this regard, the church, too, is designed to be a means of grace; therefore, she needs to acknowledge the power of the Word of God. Without rigorous teaching of the Word of God, the church can hardly function as a means of grace. Quoting Matt 28:19–20, Hodge writes, "The end to be accomplished, was the salvation of men. The means of its accomplishment was teaching."[23] True teaching leads to faithful observance of all Jesus's commandments, according to the Great Commission. Thus, again, the church needs to spend time to teach the people of God the whole gospel comprehensively. A church minister is expected to teach "that his auditors may feel the Word of God to be quick and powerful, and a discerner of the thoughts and intents of the heart."[24] The message of the church will always be relevant when it brings human beings to self-knowledge in the light of the Word. The auditors do not need political news, clichéd moral advice, or therapeutic self-help

---

21. Owen, *Works*, vol. 4, 205.
22. Owen, *Works*, vol. 4, 202–3.
23. Hodge, *Systematic Theology*, vol. 3, 467.
24. Westminster Directory for the Publick Worship of God (1645).

guidance; they need, instead, the prophetic message of the church that flows from the heart of the all-knowing God.

"The Word of God is . . . sharper than any two-edged sword, piercing to the division of soul and spirit" (Heb 4:12). Gurnall related this verse to the spiritual war between the church and her enemies.[25] The church cannot win the battle without her complete armor, one aspect of which is the Word of God. The enemies will be overcome not necessarily by destruction; they can be overcome by way of conversion. It is not the calling of the church to convert people for it is solely the work of the Holy Spirit. Yet, the church is called to go to war with the sword of the Word. A church that loses her prophetic gift fails to give eschatological direction for the society. At the end, the society will have no true hope. To be able to receive the prophetic message is to experience a foretaste of the eschatological happiness.

Thus, Hodge gives an eschatological dimension of the Scriptures when he explained the office of the Word as a means of grace:

> Hence the Scriptures so constantly represent the heavenly state, as seeing God. It is the beatific vision of the divine glory, in all its brightness, in the person of the Son of God, that purifies, ennobles, and enraptures the soul; filling all its capacities of knowledge and happiness.[26]

Hodge equates the Scriptures with light, which remains essential to vision. The Word is effective with the Spirit. It is the medium used by the Spirit to connect heaven and earth, transience and eternity, the present and the future. The Spirit transforms believers into the image of Christ "from one degree of glory to another" through "beholding the glory of the Lord" (2 Cor 3:18). Within this pneumatological context, the Scriptures has the glory and power of Christ; they refer to the glory of Christ.

Emphasizing preaching as a means of grace means that the church acknowledges the sacramental dimension of preaching. In Reformed theology, one of the principal means of grace are the sacraments. If preaching is understood as a means of grace, then we can assign a certain sacramental dimension to preaching. For P. T. Forsyth, such sacramental understanding stands in contrast with the view of preaching as a means of (mere) declaration.

25. Cf. Gurnall, *The Christian in Complete Armour*, 577.
26. Hodge, *Systematic Theology*, vol. 3, 478.

> It is only such an age that could think of preaching as something *said* with more or less force, instead of something *done* with more or less power . . . In true preaching, as in a true sacrament, more is done than said . . . The preacher . . . is a man of action . . . That is why I call him a sacramental man, not merely an expository, declaratory man. In a sacrament is there not something done, not merely shown, not merely recalled? It is no mere memorial.[27]

A sacramental view of preaching reminds us of the true evangelical spirit, namely, "not what my hands have done" but what God has done through our preaching. It reminds the church to be always dependent on the creative power of the Word.

Drawing from this sacramental view of preaching, we can see that Israel's celebration of Passover is also something done (by God) instead of something merely remembered. The event of Passover (Exod 12:1–28) is reenacted, again and ever anew, as a salvific event in the history of the church. The celebration of Passover is not a mere remembrance of God's past saving act. Whereas many church liturgies were shaped by historical events recorded in the Scriptures, in the Passover, the liturgy shaped the event itself.[28] The church is always at war with what Smith calls cultural liturgies.[29] Cultural liturgies are thick practices which are identity-shaping, get into our most fundamental desire or our most basic love. As an example, Smith describes the liturgy of the shopping mall, which we frequently consider as a neutral site, while in fact it has its own agenda in the formation of desire.[30] These cultural liturgies are not only something that humans (habitually) do; rather, they do something to us; they continually shape what we love. Contrary to these cultural liturgies is the liturgy of the church in Christian worship. Therefore, the church is called to offer meaningful liturgies that powerfully shape the direction of the human heart.[31]

---

27. Forsyth, *Positive Preaching and the Modern Mind*, 50.

28. Fretheim comments that divine act is also a liturgical event. In the Passover, God used the blood of an animal, i.e., the life of creation, to function as a sign of salvation. Yet, what is important is not the properties of the blood in itself but "the word, the promise associated with the sign, not the sign in and of itself (12:13)." Fretheim, *Exodus*, 138.

29. See Smith, *Desiring the Kingdom*, 85–86.

30. Cf. Smith, *Desiring the Kingdom*, 23–24.

31. Smith exegetes elements of church liturgy starting from the call to worship, hymn-singing, reading of the law, confession of sin, creed, prayer, sermon, baptism, eucharist, offering, and sending as practices of the kingdom that serve as meaningful counter-liturgies. Cf. Smith, *Desiring the Kingdom*, 155–214.

Throughout their history of salvation, Israel has been reminded of the story of their deliverance as the fulfilment of God's promise instead of their own creative self-liberating power. The liturgy of the Passover has also taught Israel that the community of the people of God is not more qualified than Egypt; rather, God passed over and spared Israel out of his mercy.

On one hand, though the calling of the church is to go into all the world and preach the gospel, the preacher's prime work should not be reduced to evangelizing alone while neglecting the transformation of the church.[32] On the other hand, the church should take care that she does not block the way to believe because her culture and language are no longer understood. Herbst speaks about "certain climatic conditions" for faith to arise and to grow.[33] He lists five steps, which are the church's witness of truth, her lowering of the cultural barriers, her design of safe places for those who are yet to become Christians, her offer of the liturgies for beginners, and finally her fellowship in being together, in praying and listening, in celebrating and working. These steps are worth considering for a missional strategy in the midst of "self-secularization" of the church especially in Europe.[34] Reducing the gospel to mere moral appeals has made more and more churches unattractive to society.

1.3. Aesthetic Dimension of the Word

The church can also explore the aesthetic dimension of the Scriptures. The law of the LORD is not only right and true but also "more to be desired . . . than gold . . . ; sweeter also than honey" (Ps 19:10). Aesthetic persuasion is less dogmatic for it invites rather than commands. For Calvin, this aesthetic persuasion is not possible without the mortification of the love of carnal pleasures. More importantly is Calvin's aesthetic argument, namely that love for and delight in the law must be added "so that it may not only subdue us to obedience by constraint, but also allure us by its sweetness."[35] Calvin believed that David certainly understood the law not simply as commandments, let alone as dead letter, but as the promises of God's grace.

---

32. "It is only an age engrossed with impressions and careless about realities that could regard the preacher's prime work as that of converting the world, to the neglect of transforming the Church." Forsyth, *Positive Preaching*, 50.

33. Herbst, "Minderheit mit Zukunft," 13–16.

34. Huber, "Volkskirche. Systematisch-theologisch," 249–54.

35. Calvin, *Comm*. Ps 19:10.

Defending the aesthetic argument, the contemporary philosopher Nehamas writes:

> Aesthetic judgment, I believe, never commands universal agreement, and neither a beautiful object nor a work of art ever engages a catholic community. Beauty creates smaller societies, no less important or serious because they are partial, and, from the point of view of its members, each one is orthodox—orthodox, however, without thinking of all others as heresies.[36]

Provocative as it might be, beauty is first of all something its admirers desire to share with others. Sharing, or in Christian terms *witnessing*, is less judgmental than teaching for it is freer from coercive expectation. We disagree with Nehamas on the disengagement of a catholic community since the beauty of the Word is for all the world. If it is not recognized, then it is because of sin. In reality, beauty is persuasive only for smaller communities, namely those who can appreciate true beauty. The aesthetic dimension reminds us that like beauty, truth is also persuasive only for smaller communities. From a Christian perspective we cannot possibly exclude the relation of beauty to truth and righteousness, thus also to orthodoxy, hence wherever beauty is shared it always challenges the ugly. However, beauty subtly lures people to participate in its communities of appreciation rather than imposes an 'orthodox' dogmatism.

The aesthetic dimension of the Word reminds us of its inexhaustibility. Yet, not only the Word of God has the aesthetic dimension but also its recipients. To quote Nehamas again, "Like . . . works of art, the people who matter to us are all, so far as we are concerned, inexhaustible. They always remain a step beyond the furthest point our knowledge of them has reached—though only if, and as long as, they still matter to us."[37] In Christian terms, the people who receive the Word are also 'inexhaustible' as long as we love them.[38] Nehamas is critical toward the universal character of Christian notions of agape. For him, agape discourages friendship, since in friendship we cannot love everyone the same way. Yet, he finds beauty in the teaching of Aelred of Rievaulx, who said that after the fall, Christians have friendship for Christians and agape for everyone (cf. "brotherly

---

36. Nehamas, *Only a Promise of Happiness*, 80.

37. Nehamas, *On Friendship*, 141.

38. This is not to say that humans are inexhaustible in the same sense as the Word of God, which is divine. Rather, humans are inexhaustible in a derivative sense as the objects of divine love. God inexhaustibly loves humans as the objects of his love through us.

affection" and "agape" in 2 Pet 1:7).[39] When all believers are finally united in Paradise, brotherly affection and agape will be fully reconciled. Therefore, brotherly affection, or in Nehamas's term *friendship*, is a foretaste of Paradise. In the context of theological aesthetics, Christians love (ἀγαπάω) non-believers, inviting them to join communities of appreciation, so that they can participate in shared experiences of beauty. The universal agape will then be transformed to friendship, or in biblical term *brotherly affection* (φιλαδέλφεια).

For Luke, the criterion of Christian fraternity is hearing and doing the Word of God. Jesus said, "My mother and my brothers are those who hear the Word of God and do it" (Luke 8:21). The Word's proclamation, acceptance, and practice are not disintegrated elements but belong to wholeness. The church should take care not only for the proclamation of the Word but also for its reception and exercise in the lives of the people. Similarly, in Acts we read that the Word of God was not only taught but also heard (cf. Acts 13:44; 19:10), received (11:1; 17:11), and it increased (6:7; 12:24). In Acts, we do not find the dichotomy between the objective power of the Word and the subjective reception of its hearers. Rather, the beauty of the early Christian community consists of *both* proclamation *and* reception of the Word.

1.4. Beauty: Objective or Subjective?

Whereas the ancient and medieval aesthetic theory generally advocated objectivity of beauty, later philosophers such as Hume and Kant on the contrary taught subjectivist accounts of beauty.[40] Overcoming the objective/subjective distinction, Scruton uses a kiss as an example of the experience of beauty. To kiss someone in love is "to touch the other person in his very self. Hence the kiss is compromising—it is a move from one self toward another, and a *summoning* of the other into the surface of his being."[41] Put in the ecclesiastical context, the (objective) beauty of the Word is not without

---

39. The word "brotherly affection," denotes family affection between fellow-believers, brothers and sisters in Christ (cf. Rom 12:10; 1 Thess 4:9; Heb 13:1; 1 Pet 1:22), while the word "agape" denotes the crowning virtue that encompasses all the others (cf. 2 Cor 6:6; Gal 5:22; Eph 4:2; 1 Tim 4:12; 6:11; 2 Tim 2:22; 3:10; Titus 2:2; Rev 2:19). Cf. Bauckham, *Jude, 2 Peter*, 187.

40. Cf. Hume, "Of the Standard of Taste," 136; Kant, *Critique of Judgement*, sec. 1.

41. Scruton, *Beauty*, 48.

the (subjective) appreciation of its hearers. To experience the beauty of the Word is not merely to place a part of our humanity on the Word, but to summon the Word into one's being. Bernard of Clairvaux beautifully described this happening in his mystical language:

> Yet she is not content with saying, "let him kiss me with his *mouth*," but uses the still more unusual expression, "with the *kiss* of his mouth." . . . Him, Him of Whom they prophesied—let Him speak, 'let Him kiss me with the kiss of His Mouth.' . . . For His word, 'living and efficacious,' is to me as a kiss, not indeed a contact of lips, which sometimes deceives in falsely signifying a union of hearts, but an infusion of joy, a revelation of secrets, a marvelous, and, in a sense, indistinguishable intermingling of the Light Supernal with the enlightened soul."[42]

The aesthetic mystical experience of a kiss relates intimately the beauty of the Word of Christ to the spiritual eye of the beholder. There is no objective/subjective dichotomy here but the beauty of the love relationship between Christ and his beloved bride, the church.

Overcoming such unfruitful dichotomy means that the sharing or witnessing of divine beauty in Christ can only be done within and through the church. There is always the danger of (falsely) referring to Christ alone without the participation of the church as his bride in divine beauty. Of course, the church was not loved because of her beauty. Christ does not love his bride with eros but with agape. Yet, it is precisely in this divine agape that has the power to transform the church into a beautiful bride whereby humanity can access shared experiences of true beauty. The beauty of Christ is not without his bride. We will come back later to the metaphor of bride in this book. As for this chapter, the church as the bride of Christ is the proclaimer and recipient of the Word of Christ. Karl Barth speaks of the "proclaimers and recipients of the Easter message," who "believed and responded with their confession and a life of love for Him and for the brethren."[43] As the proclaimer of the Word, the church is called to confess her bridegroom. As the recipient of the Word, she is called to live as a community of love. As there is no dichotomy between proclaiming and receiving, so we reject the dichotomy of confession and communion. A true confessing church is a loving community. Vice versa, an intimate Christian fellowship is a confessing church. In Acts, the intimate fellowship of the

---

42. Bernard, *Sermons on the Canticle of Canticles*, 4, 11–12.

43. Barth, CD III/2, 494.

believers led to them having favor with all the people and growing in numbers (cf. Acts 2:46–47). In other words, their fellowship in love was an effective confession to those outside the church. Being in an intimate fellowship did not hinder Peter and John speaking the Word of God with boldness (cf. Acts 4:29, 31). The Word of God continued to increase through the faithful preaching of the twelve and serving of the seven (cf. Acts 6:2–4, 7). The early church was a true creature of the Word of God.

2

Visible and Invisible Church

THE DISTINCTION BETWEEN VISIBLE and invisible church is a way of speaking the one church, not two separate churches. This distinction is an important one if Christians do not want to fall into either hopeless disappointment or triumphalist euphoria. It is also a *via media* between "the magical and supernatural externalism" on the one extreme and "the extravagant depreciation of all outward rites" on the other.[1] The first is the result of visibility without invisibility while the latter the result of invisibility without visibility. The two aspects of the church (visible and invisible) are rather perspectives of the one holy catholic church.

2.1. The Invisible Church

The invisible church is made up of all the elect from all ages. This invisibility is clearly taught in Ephesians. The church is the body and the fullness of Christ who fills all in all (Eph 1:22–23). The church is the realm of present salvation in which Christ's fullness is effective and powerful.[2] Thus, the church's invisibility cannot be separated from her visibility for how could one participate in this effectiveness and powerfulness of Christ's body without the visible church, "out of which there is no ordinary possibility of salvation"?[3] The Westminster Confession of Faith (WCF) understands Eph 1 as a reference to the invisible church. The church as the body and

---

1. McPherson, *Christian Dogmatics*, 417.

2. Schnelle, *Theology of the New Testament*, 566–67.

3. WCF XXV.2.

the fullness of Christ manifests in the visible oneness of the household of God, which in Ephesus consisted of Jews and Gentiles (cf. Eph 2:19). The notion of the house and family of God in Eph 2:19 is rightly discussed as a reference to the visible church in WCF. Thus, for the author of Ephesians, the church as the body of Christ becomes visible in the oneness of the household of God. Unless this invisibility manifests in the visibility, one can hardly taste the fullness of Christ.

Ephesian's body-Christology serves as a counter-alternative to the emperor cult.[4] Christ is the true peacemaker between all nations, all societal classes, and all kinds of people.

> For he himself is our peace, who has made us both one and has broken down in his flesh the dividing wall of hostility by abolishing the law of commandments expressed in ordinances, that he might create in himself one new man in place of the two, so making peace, and might reconcile us both to God in one body through the cross, thereby killing the hostility (Eph 2:14–16).

Here again, we notice that the invisibility of the one body of Christ should be made visible in the local churches. If the body-Christology was to serve as a counterculture, it should be manifested visibly in each local church in Ephesus.

The doctrine of the invisibility of the church is also the foundation for fruitful, meaningful, and sound ecumenical dialogues with churches of other theological traditions. The invisible church always transcends the local visible church. She also functions as great encouragement for the faithful and persevering sowing of the believers in the visible church for they will reap in the invisible spiritual realm. The belief of the invisibility of the church helps us to avoid confusing true works of God with mere numbers or other visible measurable results. The term *invisible* can also be interpreted as applying to the hiddenness of the church in the days of

---

4. "Against this background, the encomium tradition that echoes in the passage in 2:14–18 about Christ as the one who establishes peace can be well understood as a structurally parallel, alternative proposal to the emperor's claim as peacemaker for τὰ μφότερα [both sides]: Christ integrates Jews and Gentiles in the common realm of peace that is his own body, which at the same time is a common politeia [citizenship] (2:19b). Christ does this in such a way that those who once were Jews no longer need claim or want a special position, for they already have a privileged position (2:19ff.)." Faust, *Pax Christi et Pax Caesaris*, 475.

persecution.[5] Coherently, the invisibility of the church helps Christians not to fall into the low view of the church primarily as an external institution.

2.2. Ryle on the Visible and Invisible Church

The apostle Paul participated bodily in the churches around Ephesus; yet, his heart and vision was for the kingdom of God. In other words, he truly partook of the life of the local churches yet he sought the universal kingdom of God.[6] If Paul had merely built local churches in Ephesus, then his works has now been destroyed for Ephesus is no more. Ryle beautifully describes this creative tension when he draws true practical holiness as spiritual mindedness: "a holy man . . . will endeavor to set his affections entirely on things above, and to hold things on earth with a very loose hand."[7] There is always a danger in making the local visible church an idol, namely when we are placing false expectations on a church by pretending to be able to do what Christ alone can do.[8] The other danger is, of course, not to be visibly and bodily involved in any local church.

For Ryle, the membership of a visible church is essential to spiritual growth for in the visible church are public means of grace. Yet, Ryle also reminds us that the growth of a believer very much depends on the right manner of using these means of grace. The means can be used "in a cold and heartless way"; their "very familiarity . . . is apt to make us careless."[9] Merely participating in the visible rites can indeed lead to external religion. The remedy for this problem, according to Ryle, is to partake of public means "with our might" (Eccles 9:10). In the biblical context, doing whatever our hand finds to do with our might means enjoying life as God's given portion in his *kairos*. Thus, to miss the enjoyment of the means of grace provided by God is foolishness. Celebrating God's *kairos* is part of the understanding of the invisible aspect of the church: we do not merely participate in the means of grace externally but internally.

Ryle emphasizes the invisible church as consisting of "all true believers . . . who are really holy, and converted people . . . who have been born again

---

5. Cf. Berkhof, *Systematic Theology*, 565.

6. On the relation between church and the kingdom of God, see chap. 8.

7. Ryle, *Holiness*, 55.

8. See for instance the church in Laodicea in Rev 3:14–22.

9. Ryle, *Holiness*, 133.

and sanctified by Christ's Spirit."[10] If we use the term *holiness* to refer to those who are elected by and consecrated to the LORD, holiness is primarily an attribute of the invisible church (cf. Eph 5:27).[11] The way of worship, the form of government, and ceremonies can be different but holiness should remain the attribute of the church.[12] Despite this diversity, all the members of the church are truly holy.[13] The visible church is contingent on her holiness. She cannot and will not ignore the pursuit of holiness for God is the One who sanctifies his church. Holiness is not only the attribute of the invisible church but also the visible. For Ryle, real and practical holiness should be known by members of the true church.[14] Holiness is expected to be visibly known in the church.

2.3. A Nestorian Ecclesiology?

We should be careful that the distinction between the invisible and visible church does not reflect Nestorian ecclesiology, as has been described by Lossky.[15] The incarnation and the two natures of Christ describe a unique event and person. Moreover, every sound ecclesiology should be compatible not only with Christology, but also with anthropology and soteriology. The visibility of the church reflects her imperfect humanity, not in the sense of her wandering shadows (against Lossky), but in the sense of human sinfulness and imperfection, which is redeemed and sanctified in Christ. An ecclesiology that applies exclusively Christology to the church (read: the perfection of Christ's human nature), but fails to also apply anthropology and soteriology to ecclesiology will be led (perhaps unconsciously) to ecclesiastical self-righteousness. We should not forget that the church consists of sinful human beings who are redeemed in Christ. Just as the perfection of Christ's human nature does not deny the sinfulness and imperfection of

---

10. Ryle, *Holiness*, 307.

11. WCF XXV.1 quotes Eph 5:27 in the context of the invisible church.

12. Cf. Ryle, *Holiness*, 307–8.

13. Cf. Ryle, *Holiness*, 308.

14. Cf. Ryle, *Holiness*, 323.

15. The Eastern Orthodox theologian Vladimir Lossky speaks of a "Nestorian ecclesiology," which "would divide the Church into distinct beings: on the one hand the heavenly and invisible Church, alone true and absolute; on the other, the earthly Church (or rather "the churches") imperfect and relative, wandering in the shadows, human societies seeking to draw near, so far as is possible for them, to that transcendent perfection." Lossky, *Mystical Theology*, 186.

true believers, so Christ's human nature does not cancel the imperfection of the church (against Lossky).

As an Eastern Orthodox theologian, Lossky teaches a theandric organism: "all that can be asserted or denied about Christ can equally well be applied to the Church."[16] We can affirm Lossky's theandric organism of the church with regard to Christology but only to a certain extent. We should not neglect the organic relation between ecclesiology and anthropology, more precisely, between the doctrine of the church and the doctrine of *humanity and sin*. The doctrine of humanity and sin safeguards the church from the danger of self-righteousness claiming her infallibility and perfection; the church is the bride of Christ; she is not Christ. The former assures the certainty of the progressive sanctification of the church as the work of God who is faithful. In this context, the teaching of the two aspects of the church should be understood from the perspective of the dialectic between Christology and anthropology. The theandric relation in Christology is not equivalent to the relation of ecclesiology and anthropology. Ecclesiology is anthropology in the state of grace. In relation to Christology, the church should indeed reflect the beauty of Christ's human nature or human will which "follows . . . as subject to his divine and omnipotent will."[17] Just as that of Christian believers, the progressive sanctification of the church is a lifelong process. The visible church does not struggle to an ideal perfection with her own strength. On the contrary, the visible church attains her redemption in Christ alone.

Christologically perceived, the visibility of the church is not an aspect divided from her invisibility. Following Chalcedonian Christology, these two aspects should be unconfused, unchangeable, indivisible, and inseparable. Indivisible and inseparable mean both aspects are two ways of speaking the one holy catholic church.

We should discuss the properties of each aspect. According to the WCF, the invisible aspect of the church is related to her electedness, being the spouse of Christ, and being the fullness of Christ who fills all in all (cf. Eph 1:23).[18] The church's electedness is the firm foundation of her everlastingness, especially in the midst of persecution and tribulation. The gates of hell shall not prevail against her. Her electedness is not something

16. Lossky, *Mystical Theology*, 187.

17. The Third Council of Constantinople: The Definition of Faith, in *NPNF* II/14, ed. Schaff & Wace, 345.

18. WCF XXV.1.

that should make the church proud or boast her superiority for such is alien to the right understanding of election in Reformed tradition. Being the spouse of Christ the church is called to be the faithful recipient of divine love while loving her children just like Christ has loved her. Being the fullness of Christ the church is to be governed by Christ. On Eph 1:23 Calvin commented, "though all things are regulated by the will and power of Christ, yet the subject of which Paul particularly speaks is the spiritual government of the church."[19]

The WCF relates the visibility of the church with her profession of the true religion, being the kingdom of Christ, being the house of God, out of which there is no ordinary possibility of salvation.[20] Against docetic ecclesiology, the church should be visibly seen through her profession of the true religion, i.e. true reverence of God joined with love of God.[21] This also includes right teaching of the doctrine of the gospel, right administration of divine ordinances, and right performance of public worship, as taught in the WCF. Being the kingdom of Christ the church should gather fish of every kind (cf. Matt 13:47), increase peace on earth, and uphold the kingdom with justice and righteousness (cf. Isa 9:7). Being the household of God the fellowship of the church's citizens that overcomes hostility and alienation should be visibly seen (cf. Eph 2:16, 19). Finally, the visibility of the church should be revealed in the growth of the number of believers (cf. Acts 2:47).[22]

We should take care to teach neither over-realized nor under-realized eschatology applied to ecclesiology. Escaping from the responsibility of the visible unity of the church to the invisible realm, for instance, is a form of under-realized eschatology for it does not take seriously the visible aspect of the church. As has been mentioned in the previous paragraph, the reality of salvation *in* the church, the reality of the church as God's household and as Christ's kingdom, and the church's profession of true religion should not be reduced to a mere phantasm.

Finally, with regard to indivisibility and inseparableness the church should be critical of a Nestorian ecclesiology. A Nestorian model separates and divides the one church into two unrelated beings. She is not the one and

19. Calvin, *Comm.* Eph 1:23.

20. WCF XXV.2.

21. Cf. Calvin, *Inst.* I.2.1.

22. The WCF beautifully relates the fact that outside of the visible church there is no ordinary possibility of salvation to visible church growth in Acts 2:47.

same church on earth and in heaven but rather two separate ecclesiastical beings. A Nestorian ecclesiology fails to explain the oneness of the church for it can only put the two aspects of the church in sharp opposition. The paradoxical tension will finally result in incoherence and contradiction. In this case, the invisible aspect will always be opposed to the visible aspect.

The Chalcedonian ecclesiology, on the contrary, will equally emphasize the visible aspect of the church, so that she can testify to the mystery of incarnation. The church is one and she is invisible and visible. Like her bridegroom, the church should take the form of a servant. The visible aspect of the church does not have its own being, but is in the being of the one holy catholic church. What is the implication and application of this Chalcedonian model? It helps the church to avoid the old Christological heresies that can reappear in ecclesiological models.

According to dyothelite Christology, Christ has two wills (divine and human). This doctrine is in coherence with Chalcedonian Christology that teaches the two natures in Christ. Lossky applies this dyothelite Christology in his understanding of the sacraments that, he believes, "admit of two wills and of two operations taking place simultaneously."[23] The church should be able to differentiate that the will of the church office-bearers (Lossky mentions the priest and the bishop) is not automatically the will of God. Equating the will or the operation of the church office-bearers with the divine will is highly problematic.[24] In Gethsemane, Christ surrendered his (human) will to the will of the Father (cf. Matt 26:39). Attacking Monothelitism, Calvin commented on this verse:

> But if even Christ was under the necessity of holding his will captive, in order to subject it to the government of God, though it was properly regulated, how carefully ought we to repress the violence of our feelings, which are always inconsiderate, and rash, and full of rebellion?[25]

Calvin used *argumentum a maiore ad minus* (argument from greater to less) to warn us how much more we should be critical against our own will. Even Christ's human will is not identical with our sinful will. The same

---

23. Lossky, *Mystical Theology*, 187.

24. There is a danger of assuming that the teaching of the church is the law of God. The Christological application to ecclesiology is more likely to introduce this erroneous teaching.

25. Calvin, *Comm.* Matt 26:39.

principle applies to ecclesiology: the church should be able to differentiate the will of her office-bearers from the will of God (against Lossky).

The church is called to give up her own will to God's disposal in Christ. Only then will we have the union in Christ between divine will and the will of the church, between divine operation and the operation of the church. To draw again from the WCF, subjecting the visible aspect to the invisible aspect also means that the church's electedness, as being the invisible aspect, should have signs in the visible aspect. In other words, the visibility of the church is the mark of her electedness. Thus, we can understand the right teaching of the gospel, the right administration of divine ordinances, and the right performance of public worship, as taught in the WCF, as true marks of the church's electedness. Just as in Reformed soteriology we speak of the true marks of the elect, here we speak of the true marks of the church's electedness in ecclesiology.

The will of the church to be the kingdom of Christ should always be subject to the will of God for the church as the spouse of Christ. Without this subjection, the church's visible aspect will be understood erroneously. Thus, for instance, the concept of the church as the kingdom of Christ without the subjection of the church to Christ as her bridegroom will destroy the true feminine beauty of the church. On one side, the church is not called to exercise masculine power in society. She is rather called to witness the righteous kingship of Christ both in her community and on earth. On the other side, she is not to be discouraged by the highly secular society as with Christ and his fullness, she is entrusted to rule and to fill all in all (cf. Eph 1:23 cited in the WCF). The church shares in the power of Christ to be fishers of men, to increase peace on earth, and to uphold the kingdom with righteousness. The femininity of the church as the spouse of Christ is an important criterion to test whether her visible aspect of being the kingdom of Christ is understood biblically or erroneously. We will discuss the church's femininity in relation to Christ as her bridegroom in more detail in the next chapter.

Finally, the church should execute the will to overcome hostility and alienation, the will to grow in the number of believers in order to testify her subjection to the will of God for the church as the household of God, out of which no ordinary possibility of salvation is available. It is noteworthy that the WCF locates the ordinary possibility of salvation in the visible aspect.[26]

26. Calvin commented on Acts 2:47, the verse cited in the WCF to explain the visible aspect of the church, with the belief that salvation is not out of the visible church:

The participation in the invisible church is certainly necessary for salvation, for the WCF uses salvific language for the invisible aspect. The availability of salvation in the visible church is not without the true fellowship in the household of God (cf. Eph 2:19) that results in the growth of number of believers (cf. Acts 2:42–47). Carefully said, the growth of number was not the result of sophisticated strategies of evangelism but the genuine Christian fellowship of the early church. This fellowship includes devotion to the apostle's teaching, the breaking of bread, prayers, wonders done through the apostles, alms, worship, and having favor with all people. The genuine fellowship of the early church was visible in a multifaceted testimony.

2.4. Reformed Confessions

Like the WCF, the Second Helvetic Confession briefly mentions the term *invisible* for the church, because "being hidden from our eyes and known only to God," the church "often secretly escapes human judgment."[27] The Second Helvetic Confession cites 2 Tim 2:19, "The Lord knows those who are his." In this verse, the invisibility of the church is immediately related to a true mark of a believer, i.e. the departure from iniquity. The description in the Second Helvetic Confession came from Zwingli who wrote that the church "is called invisible not as if they that believe were invisible, but because it is not evident to human eyes who do believe."[28] Zwingli understood the holy city as the invisible church coming down from heaven (cf. Rev 21:2). With this reference, we can conclude that for Zwingli, the invisible aspect of the church should be understood eschatologically. At the eschaton, the invisible church will be fully revealed.

In a similar tenor, Calvin also taught that in the visible church "many hypocrites . . . are tolerated for a time" until the final judgment.[29] He also cited 2 Tim 2:19 to support the invisible aspect of the church.[30] In his

---

"Furthermore, we must note that he saith, that those were gathered unto the Church which should be saved. For he teacheth that this is the means to attain salvation, if we be incorporate into the Church. For like as there is no remission of sins, so neither is there any hope of salvation." Calvin, *Comm.* Acts 2:47.

27. Second Helvetic Confession, XVII.

28. Zwingli, "A Short and Clear Exposition of the Christian Faith," in *Latin Works*, vol. 2, 260.

29. Calvin, *Inst.* IV.1.7.

30. Cf. Calvin, *Inst.* IV.1.8.

commentary, Calvin understood this verse to be the source of comfort when "unexpected events" took place for God is satisfied with the number of the elect.[31] When the church seems to appear very small, the doctrine of the invisible church shall become the comfort for true believers.

Thus, according to the Belgic Confession, the "holy Church is preserved or supported by God against the rage of the whole world; though she sometimes (for a while) appear very small, and, in the eyes of man, to be reduced to nothing: as during the perilous reign of Ahab, when nevertheless *the Lord reserved unto him seven thousand men, who had not bowed their knees to Ba'al.*"[32] The Belgic Confession had the visible church in mind. She does not always appear powerfully in the human eyes.

The invisible aspect of the church remains coherent with the hiddenness of Christ's divinity in his humiliation yet it will be revealed in his exaltation. His divine power was concealed by the humble form of his servanthood. Consequently, the church is called to persevere in her humble and vulnerable service to the world while being content with her invisible character known solely by the LORD. Only then will the church be faithful to the *theologia crucis* instead of *theologia gloriae*.

2.5. The Church Militant and Triumphant

Similarly but not identically, we can speak also of church militant and church triumphant. It is not to be understood as two churches but as one holy catholic church. The glory of the church is reserved at the *eschaton* while here on earth the church is to suffer with Christ. The church is to wrestle "against the cosmic powers over this present darkness, against the spiritual forces of evil in the heavenly places" (Eph 6:12). The church is militant when she partakes of spiritual warfare. In the context of Ephesians it was warfare to break down "the dividing wall of hostility" creating one new man in Christ (2:14). Thus, church militant is the hope for true unity of the church. When the church stops breaking down the separating wall, she does not reflect the unity of the body of her bridegroom.

We can view the relation between church militant and church triumphant both from the perspective of Lukan and Johannine writings. In Lukan writings, the way of Christ to Jerusalem is understood as the way

---

31. Calvin, *Comm.* 2 Tim 2:19.

32. Belgic Confession, Art. 27.

from suffering to glory (cf. Luke 24:26; Acts 14:22).[33] From this perspective, church militant must precede church triumphant. While on earth, the church remains in her state of suffering, fight, and struggle. Church triumphant is reserved for eschatology, i.e. when Christ will come again triumphantly. The most important virtues here are patience and faith. In Johannine writings, crucifixion can be understood *as* glorification.[34] In other words, suffering *is* glory. From this perspective, the church militant is the church triumphant even here and now on earth. The church is already triumphant, because she does not buy the narrative of worldly power and glory but readily and joyfully suffers for the sake of Christ. On the contrary, the church is defeated when she does not bear her cross faithfully. A suffering church is a triumphant church.

2.6. Webster on Spiritual Visibility

Despite the pervasiveness of the visibility of the church in contemporary ecclesiology, Webster has argued for the invisibility, or in other words, the *spiritual* visibility of the church. According to Webster, the church's active life should not be understood as a visible realization, even a realization of the presence of God, but "as an attestation of the perfect work of God in Christ, . . . effective in the Spirit's power."[35] For Webster, the church's attestations of God reflect a systematic explanation of Chalcedonian Christology: God's perfection and human activity are neither separated nor confused.[36] However, unlike Lossky who insists on a dyothelite ecclesiology as an application of the dyothelite Christology, Webster moves in a direction of a typical evangelical theology, namely that salvation is by grace alone in Christ's redemption. Thus the distinctive character of evangelical ecclesiology must be the church's faithful reference to the perfect work of Christ. Webster rejects any kind of synthesis of Christology and ecclesiology because of the qualitative difference between Christ and the objects of his mercy.[37] His

33. Cf. Schnelle, *Theology of the New Testament*, 484.

34. Cf. Schnelle, *Theology of the New Testament*, 700–701.

35. Webster, "On Evangelical Ecclesiology," 24.

36. "This combination of emphases, on the 'spiritual visibility' of the church, and on the character of its acts as 'attestations' of God, reflects an orderly account of the relation between God's perfection and creaturely being and activity, *neither separating nor confusing* the divine and the human." Webster, "On Evangelical Ecclesiology," 24; italics mine.

37. Cf. Webster, "On Evangelical Ecclesiology," 23.

rejection is based on his insistence on an evangelical theology that should teach the completeness of Christ's perfection in itself.

We want to explore Webster's insistence on the spiritual character of the church's visibility. Such a visible aspect cannot be understood as the church's self-realization, whether with regard to her strive for unity, holiness, catholicity, or apostolicity. Rather, the church is called to attest to the perfect unity of the body of Christ, the perfect holiness of Christ, the perfect universality of the cosmic Christ, and the perfect sending of Christ. Is this rhetoric of indication a kind of avoidance of the church's responsibility and activity, a kind of excuse or even self-justification for the church's passivity and imperfection? "Don't look at me for I am imperfect; look at Jesus alone!" Webster reminds us that attestation is also activity.[38] The church does not lose her visibility when she does not speak on her own authority, but whatever she hears she speaks and declares in the power of the Spirit (cf. John 16:13). On the contrary, when the church keeps referring to herself, she will lose her true visibility. The incarnate Christ is the image of the invisible God (cf. Col 1:15). Christ faithfully refers to the Father. So is the church called to be the image of Christ who faithfully refers and attests to the invisible Christ in heaven.

As the image of the invisible God, Christ created all things, "in heaven and on earth, visible and invisible" (Col 1:16). In this verse, visible and invisible are perceived within the theology of creation. There is a shift in focus, however, from creation to the church in the transitional stanza of 1:17–18a.[39] This shift permits us to relate the creation of all things visible and invisible to ecclesiology. In Paul's thought, churches on earth are manifestations of the heavenly church. Thus, both heavenly and earthly, visible and invisible church was created by Christ. Not only were all things created by Christ, but all things, visible and invisible church included, also hold together in him (cf. Col 1:17). The church's invisible aspect should not be understood in a platonic sense. When we say the church has an invisible aspect, we mean that the spiritual treasures of the church are hidden in Christ. The life of the church is also hidden with Christ (cf. Col 3:3). Only if we understand rightly the church's invisibility, we will be freed from the false notion of the church's visibility.

38. Cf. Webster, "On Evangelical Ecclesiology," 29.

39. For three different proposals concerning the structure of stanzas in Col 1:15–20, see Moo, *Colossians and Philemon*, 115–16.

Webster's rhetoric of attestation can safeguard erroneous concepts of the church's visibility. Our local church may have become an idol when she tries to be what Christ alone can be. She can become an idol when we see the sign of measuring God's work by the degree of what Christopherson calls "brand advancement."[40] When buildings and budgets become the primary measurement of church success then the visibility of the church is understood in an erroneous way. Christ was not successful because he owned big church buildings, established powerful ecclesial institution or Christian political parties.[41] He was triumphant and victorious in his sacrificial death on the cross. The church's attestation to the sacrifice of Christ, her calling to sacrificial life should remain visible. Just as the Devil tempted Christ in the wilderness by showing him all the kingdoms of the world and their glory, the church always faces the same temptation to be given the glory of the worldly kingdoms. The church's visibility, however, is to reflect the glory of the kingdom of God, not the worldly kingdoms.

Far from reflecting a Nestorian ecclesiology, the invisible and visible aspects of the church might be compared to the words of Scripture read in worship, which are "symbols in the realistic sense of the word: material signs of the presence of the spiritual world."[42] Like the sacrament, the church herself signifies an admission into a mystery, i.e. the manifestation of an invisible heavenly reality which is always present in the visible church. The church is a *symbolon* in the Greek sense: she brings two things together, namely her visible and invisible aspects. In the modern sense, the church is a visible sign of something invisible, of God's gracious election, of the headship of Christ, of the church's spiritual marriage and her fulness, of faith, hope, and love, which represent the essence of the church.[43] The church is a mystery as in her visible aspect the hidden mystery of the Word of God has been made fully known and revealed (cf. Col 1:24–26). The heavenly church manifests herself in the earthly visible church. The church must be reformed according to Christ alone.

---

40. Jeff Christopherson, "Five Signs My Church May Have Become an Idol." *Christianity Today*, 5 August 2020, https://www.christianitytoday.com/edstetzer/2018/october/five-signs-church-become-idol-jeff-christopherson-missio-mo.html.

41. I owe this autocritique to my dear spiritual mentor Rev Dr. Stephen Tong.

42. Lossky, *Mystical Theology*, 189.

43. Cf. WCF XXV.1; see also Pictet, *Christian Theology*, 430.

3

Metaphors for the Church

THE SCRIPTURES DESCRIBE THE church with metaphors. Postmodern philosophers such as Ricoeur see metaphorical language as the main vehicle
for the expression of forms of meaning rather than objectifying engagement.[1] The ambiguity of the metaphor is actually considered to have the
power to explain the multiplicity of aspects or dimensions of a reality. The
truth of a metaphor is more a matter of disclosure than a matter of coherence with reality. There is a paradox within a metaphorical attribute, so that
when we assert X is Y, at the same time we claim that X is not Y. Despite
being ornamental, metaphors make real claims about reality that goes beyond propositional forms.[2] Despite its paradoxical nature, we believe that
the biblical metaphors for the church are not incoherent one with another.
In his book *Images of the Church in the New Testament*, Minear believes
that the great mystery of the church requires a kaleidoscopic study.[3] In
this chapter, we are going to look at some metaphors of the church such as
family, building, holy temple, field, bride, body of Christ, and vine.

3.1. The Family of God

In the New Testament, the church as God's family was a *status confessionis*
against Roman society, in which one's family background was foundational

1. Cf. Ricoeur, *The Rule of Metaphor*.

2. Cf. Paul, "Metaphor," in Vanhoozer, *Dictionary for Theological Interpretation*,
507–8.

3. Cf. Minear, *Images of the Church*, 226–27.

for one's status, while in the church, the distinctions based on race, family, and gender did not matter anymore.[4] Such inclusivity or openness is even regarded as one of the most important reasons for the success of early Christianity.[5] While the world is struggling and doomed to fail in the issue of racism, the church is called to witness her community as the family of God. The failure in the society reflects the failure of the church to be salt and light of the world. Especially when the sacramental practice becomes the way of life, the church will be a witness as a creative counterculture for the society. "There is neither Jew nor Greek, there is neither slave nor free, there is no male and female, for you are all one in Christ Jesus," wrote Paul (Gal 3:28). Those who were baptized have put on Christ and Christ is one.

Family is something that is given, not something that we choose. Not only is showing partiality forbidden in a family (cf. Jas 2:1, 9), it is even impossible to build a family based on partiality. The character of givenness, therefore, is constitutive of familial life. We do not choose to be children of God; rather, it is God who chose us to be his family. The church as family is a new community initiated by God himself. Human choice is subjectively preferential while God's election is unconditional. The unconditionality of God's election is manifested when he "chose what is foolish in the world to shame the wise; God chose what is weak in the world to shame the strong; God chose what is low and despised in the world, even things that are not, to bring to nothing things that are, so that no human being might boast in the presence of God . . . Let the one who boasts, boast in the Lord" (1 Cor 1:27–29, 31). In the context of Pauline *theologia crucis*, that is, the reversal motif of the kingdom of God, we read that the church is a truly radically new community unlike the (old) communities of the world, which prefer the wise, the strong, and what is high. In other words, there is a certain social criticism in the image of the church as family.

What constitutes who belongs to the family of God is not biological ties but doing the will of God (cf. Mark 3:31–35).[6] The church as familial *koinonia* means that she is united in the same will and the same mind. The term *family* can be legitimately used where a communal entity is characterized by "common character."[7] Though each local church, even each member of a local church, could have a particular calling, the church has

---

4. Cf. Schnelle, *Theology of the New Testament*, 330.

5. Cf. Ebel, *Die Attraktivität früher christlicher Gemeinden.*

6. Cf. Schnelle, *Theology of the New Testament*, 404.

7. Minear, *Images of the Church*, 166–67.

the same universal narrative to be lived, for a family is characterized by common narrative. Being one family means living one narrative of the gospel. Paul exhorted the Galatians to do good generally to everyone and "especially to those who are of the household of faith" (Gal 6:10). An elder or overseer should manage his own household before he can be entrusted to care for God's church as the household of God (cf. 1 Tim 3:4–5). At the household of God, the judgment of God will begin (cf. 1 Pet 4:17). Peter related this judgment to the true and false suffering. The household of God is characterized by true suffering, which is suffering according to God's will, for the name of Christ.

3.2. God's Building

Another metaphor for the church is that of a building. The church as building (Lat.: *aedificatio*; Gr.: οἰκοδομή) means that she is edified or built up by Christ. In 1 Cor 3:10–15, the range of meanings includes God who gives the grace, Jesus Christ as the foundation, the apostle as a skilled master builder, what sort of materials one uses for construction, and finally the final test of the building by fire. "According to the grace of God" means that the church is not a self-built institution, but God's given. Any effort to build the church by one's own strength, wisdom, and strategy is doomed to fail. "Given to me, like a skilled master builder" means that we are entrusted to participate in the edification of his church. "With gold, silver, precious stones, wood, hay, straw" means that there is different sort of materials that can be used for building the church. Calvin interpreted *gold, silver, precious stones* as "doctrine worthy of Christ" whereas *wood, hay, straw* means "a mass of strange doctrines."[8] Minear understands true edification as something that goes beyond moral improvement: "Whatever edifies the brother does far more than improve his moral behavior; it strengthens him in his position in this structured society."[9] In this context, *gold, silver, precious stones* can be interpreted as helping the members of the church find and fulfil their particular callings and functions within the ecclesial grand narrative (see also 1 Cor 12:14–20). Finally, "it will be revealed by fire" means that not every superstructure will survive on the Judgment Day. Calvin spoke of "vain ambition" that will be exposed by divine light.[10] For the good and faithful

---

8. Calvin, *Comm.* 1 Cor 3:12.

9. Minear, *Images of the Church*, 164.

10. "For ambition is blind—man's favor is blind—the world's applause is blind, but

master builders, however, this verse is a source of comfort and encouragement, knowing that how they build upon the holy foundation was always known by God and will be rewarded at the end.

Very close to the building metaphor is the metaphor of field (1 Cor 3:6–9). Here, Paul emphasized the servanthood of both himself and Apollos. God's servants can have different roles but he who gives the growth is God alone. God's servants are one and fellow workers, not competitors. Each servant of God will receive his/her own wages from God. Understanding the church as God's field means rejecting the idea that she is human field or is given the growth by humans.

In Romans, Paul made building on no one else's foundation his ambition (cf. Rom 15:20). For him, it means to preach the gospel where Christ has not yet been named. One of the churches that Paul founded was the church in Ephesus. Built on the foundation of the apostles and prophets, the saints in Ephesus, both Jews and Gentiles, were members of the household of God (cf. Eph 2:19–20). When Paul wrote about the whole structure that grows into a holy temple, being built together into God's dwelling place, he revealed the close relation between the building metaphor and the temple metaphor.

In First Peter, the building metaphor was based on Christology: Christ is a living stone, a cornerstone who was rejected by men yet believed by elect exiles of the Dispersion (cf. 1 Pet 2:4, 6). Christ the living stone was chosen and precious in the sight of God. Likewise, elect exiles of the Dispersion were also chosen according to the foreknowledge of God for obedience to Christ (cf. 1 Pet 1:1–2). Through Christ, they, like living stones were "being built up as a spiritual house, to be a holy priesthood, to offer spiritual sacrifices acceptable to God" (1 Pet 2:5). Here too, there is a close relation between the building metaphor and the temple metaphor, for the spiritual house is none other than the new temple, the holy priesthood the community of the temple, the spiritual sacrifices the offerings in the new temple.[11]

3.3. A Holy Temple

In Ephesians, the metaphor of structure (οἰκοδομή) is closely related to holy temple "in whom [Christ Jesus] the whole structure, being joined together,

---

this darkness God afterwards dispels in his own time." Calvin, *Comm.* 1 Cor 3:13.

11. Cf. Jobes, *1 Peter*, 148.

grows into a holy temple in the Lord" (Eph 2:21). In this verse, we read a mixture of metaphors as well as a dynamic process. The church as building is an ongoing process into a holy temple. Lincoln reminds us that since in the Old Testament prophecy, all nations would come to worship God and be taught by God in the Jerusalem temple, the temple motif in Ephesians is possibly understood as the fulfilment of the Old Testament prophecy: "It is possible that for a Jew such a notion would recall the vision of eschatological peace which would prevail when the Gentiles joined Israel in worship in the temple in Zion, a vision found in Isa 2:2–4 and Mic 4:1–4, although there is no conscious effort to invoke such prophecies here."[12] We are now at the end time when these Old Testament promises are fulfilled. The concept of "already" does not negate the concept of "not yet" in Eph 2:21. The church is predestined to be the new temple, where all nations and races will gather to worship and to know the LORD.

Other than in Ephesians, the metaphor of holy temple can be found in First Corinthians and the Gospel of John. The church is God's temple for God's Spirit dwells in the church (cf. 1 Cor 3:16). The sacredness of the temple is to be respected so that God will destroy anyone who destroys it. Note, that the temple in v. 17 is understood in a communal instead of an individual sense. Though it is not wrong to say that God's Spirit also dwells in each believer (cf. 1 Cor 6:19), 1 Cor 3:16–17 make clear that it is about a communal indwelling of the Spirit of God.[13] What are the implications? First, the destruction of the temple in v. 17 has to be understood more as destroying a Christian community rather than an individual believer. Secondly, the Corinthians were warned that their faith should not rest in the wisdom of men or of this world (cf. 1 Cor 2:4–5; 3:19) for those who boasted in men would create division, thus destroying God's holy temple. Thirdly, the remedy for this destruction is to understand that servants of God belong to Christian community, not vice versa (cf. 1 Cor 3:21–22). Paul or Apollos or Cephas belonged to the Corinthians, yet the Corinthians belonged to Christ, and Christ to God (cf. 1 Cor 3:23). A healthy church does not belong to a human leader or owner for Christ is the head of the church. Office-bearers in the church are servants who belong to the temple of God, i.e. the church. Finally, the Christian community does not rule over the servants of God but belong to Christ. In this understanding, God preserves the unity of his church in Christ.

12. Lincoln, *Ephesians*, 140.

13. Cf. Thiselton, *The First Epistle to the Corinthians*, 316.

The metaphor of the body of each believer as a temple of the Spirit in 1 Cor 6:19 is governed by the concept of divine ownership. "You are not your own, for you were bought with a price" (1 Cor 6:19–20). Whereas in 1 Cor 3 the whole congregation is called a temple (cf. 1 Cor 3:16–17), in 1 Cor 6 the body of each individual believer in the church is called a temple. The individual application of the temple of the Spirit lies in the flight from sexual immorality, which is a sin against one's own body (v. 18). Against this sin of fornication, Calvin wrote, "but *fornication* leaves a stain impressed upon the body, such as is not impressed upon it from other sins."[14] Other sins do not directly affect the body; fornication does. Yet, the body of a believer is a temple of the Spirit. Everyone who takes seriously the sacredness of the Spirit's temple guards one's body from sexual immorality. Paul closed his entire argument with a doxological command. Just as in the temple God is glorified, so too God should be glorified in the body of every individual believer. In another letter Paul wrote that it meant presenting believer's "bodies as a living sacrifice, . . . which is your spiritual worship" (Rom 12:1). Whereas in First Corinthians the image of the temple leads to a doxological command to glorify God in the body, in Romans presenting the bodies ends with a temple image. The holy temple is inseparable from the body of the believer. The church as holy temple means that she is the place where the bodies of believers are presented as a holy sacrifice to God.

The image of temple can also be found in the Gospel of John. Jesus spoke about the temple of his body, prophesying his resurrected body as the new temple (cf. John 2:18–22). In John 4, the Fourth Evangelist again announces that Jesus will replace the worship on Mt. Gerizim and in Jerusalem (cf. John 4:21). The worship in Spirit and truth is no other than true worship in Jesus, the new temple. There is a strong relation between Jesus's cleansing of the temple and his human body as the fulfilment of the temple typology.[15] Unlike the Old Testament people, we do not look forward to the fulfilment of this typology. It is already fulfilled in the resurrected Jesus. How do we benefit from this understanding? That the centrality of Christ as *the* mediation between God and human should relativize the church. The church is a mediation only in so far as she lets herself always be cleansed by Christ. The church is not the mediation in herself. Rather, she reflects

14. Calvin, *Comm.* 1 Cor 6:18.

15. Carson writes, "Jesus cleansed the temple; under this typological reading of the Old Testament, he also replaced it, fulfilling its purposes." Carson, *Gospel according to John*, 145.

the mediation of Christ, the fulfilment of the Old Testament temple theology. Just like true worship of the Father in John 4 relativizes the idea of localizing and limiting the presence of God, whether in Mt. Gerizim or in Jerusalem, so the church's confession on the exclusive mediation of Christ should relativize any idea of ecclesiocentrism.[16]

3.4. The Bride of Christ

The church is also called the bride of Christ. The metaphor of marital relation can be found in Matthean, Johannine, and Pauline writings. Because this image appears only in four New Testament writings, Minear categorizes it as belonging to minor images.[17] In 2 Cor 11:1–6. Paul warned about the danger of receiving a different spirit or a different gospel that would lead astray the thoughts of the Corinthians from a sincere devotion to Christ as the serpent deceived Eve. Such deception could be the effect of the Corinthian's accusations of Paul's insincerity (cf. 2 Cor 1:12). In Eph 5:22–31, the bride metaphor is closely related to submission and sanctification. The church submits to and is sanctified by Christ. The church's subjection is a response to the sacrificial love of Christ. The more and the deeper the church understands Christ's sacrificial love, the more she will submit to her husband.

We can also find the bride metaphor in the Parable of the Ten Virgins (Matt 25:1–13). Matthew related the bride/virgin metaphor to watchfulness. The church does not know the day of the bridegroom's coming. In ecclesial context, the oil can be interpreted as steadfast zeal for the kingdom of God. On this parable, Calvin rightly commented, "the plain and natural meaning of the whole is, that it is not enough to have ardent zeal for a short time, if we have not also a constancy that never tires."[18] The rise of secularism in the West cannot be denied. Rather than being discouraged or falling into self-pity, the church as the bride of Christ must maintain her holy zeal for the kingdom.

---

16. John does not make direct connection between the temple and the church, yet a contemporary application of his teaching on the mediation of Christ can include the rejection of ecclesiocentrism.

17. Minear, *Images of the Church*, 56.

18. Calvin, *Comm.* Matt 25:1.

In Revelation, the church was described as ideal city, whose eschato-logical counterpart was the unholy city Babylon.[19] When Babylon will be destroyed, "the voice of bridegroom and bride will be heard . . . no more" (Rev 18:23). Though this verse does not directly refer to the church but rather to voice of gladness,[20] we can interpret this verse as divine judgment upon worldly city once occupied by luxuries and pleasures, because she had persecuted the people of God by removing their joys of life. As long as the church is on earth, she is called to faithfully persevere in the midst of persecution by the worldly city such as Babylon. Yet, God will vindicate his bride by destroying his enemies.

In sharp opposition to the unholy city of Babylon, the holy city of new Jerusalem was seen by John as a bride prepared and adorned for her husband (cf. Rev 21:2). Again, we read the motif of the absence of gladness here. God "will wipe away every tear from their eyes" (21:4). The bride metaphor for the church is more connected to lamentation; her gladness is reserved eschatologically when her husband will return. It also refers to the intimate communion and relationship between God and his redeemed people. In Rev 21:1–4, the bride metaphor coalesces with the tabernacle theology and covenant theology: God's dwelling place is with mortals; they will be his people and he will be their God. We agree with Minear that the bride metaphor did not by itself form the determinative pattern.[21] God showed John the bride having the glory of God, that is, his "tabernacling presence with his people, which clothes them."[22] Here, again, the bride metaphor is placed within the context of tabernacle theology.

Finally, the church as the bride of Christ and the Spirit pray for the coming of the bridegroom (cf. Rev 22:17). It is in the power of the Spirit that the church can participate in the waiting upon the coming of Christ. Here, the bride metaphor coalesces with pneumatology. We cannot prop-erly understand the metaphor of bride without various biblical theologies, in whose contexts this metaphor lies.

---

19. Cf. Schnelle, *Theology of the New Testament*, 767–768.

20. Cf. Jer 25:10; see also Beale, *The Book of Revelation*, 920–921.

21. Minear, *Images of the Church*, 56.

22. Beale, *Book of Revelation*, 1066.

3.5. The Body of Christ

The next metaphor for the church is that of the body of Christ. This image or metaphor is used to describe the church in the Pauline corpus. In First Corinthians, Paul explicitly identified the church with the body of Christ: "Now you are the body of Christ and individually members of it" (1 Cor 12:27). The individual member participates in the body of Christ through the Lord's Supper (cf. 1 Cor 10:16). The members are many and yet one body (cf. 1 Cor 10:17; 12:12). The unity of the body relativizes ethnic and social differences: Jews or Greeks, slaves or free, all were baptized into one body (cf. 12:13). Paul listed the obstacles for this unity of the body: self-exclusion (cf. 1 Cor 12:15–16), uniformity (cf. 12:17), and self-sufficiency (cf. 12:21). Corresponding to the diversity of members are the many spiritual gifts in the church (cf. 12:27–30). Unity of the body does not discourage diversity; on the contrary, it is only meaningful if the diversity is assumed. Without diversity there will be no unity but only uniformity. The metaphor of the body of Christ encourages the church not only to accept but also to promote diversity (of callings and spiritual gifts).

Similarly, Paul reminded the Romans that many members of the body "do not all have the same function" (Rom 12:4). They should therefore use the different gifts given to each. Since they are one body in Christ, they belong one to another (cf. 12:5). Knowing one's particular gift and using it faithfully for the body of Christ is the meaning of thinking "with sober judgment . . . according to the measure of faith" (12:3). As an implication, a local church is also called to know her particular calling and to fulfil it as a member of the one body. Just as the body of Christ is one even though it has many gifts, so different local churches may have different callings but there is only one universal church. Because believers are one body in Christ, Paul appealed to them to present their bodies as a living sacrifice. Just as baptism does not constitute the body of Christ, so sacrifice does not constitute his body but is made possible by this pre-given reality.[23]

In the Christocentrism of Colossians, the church is also called the body of Christ (cf. Col 1:18, 24). From Christ, the Head, the whole body is nourished; not holding fast to Christ, the true wisdom, the Colossians could be led astray by false wisdom such as the promotion of self-made religion, false asceticism, worship of angels, and boasting about visions (cf. 2:18–19, 23). This false philosophy cannot be peacefully reconciled with Christian

---

23. Cf. Schnelle, *Theology of the New Testament*, 331.

faith. On the contrary, the Colossians were called in one body to the peace of Christ (cf. 3:15). Thus, the author of Colossians warned the church as the body of Christ not only about the danger of false wisdom but also of false peace, i.e. worldly syncretism between false philosophy and Christian faith. The remedy is the belief in the cosmic rule, the preeminence of Christ.

Schnelle has pointed out that the body of Christ metaphor accentuates "the priority of Christology to ecclesiology."[24] This is clearly attested not only in Colossians but also in Ephesians. The church, which is the body of Christ, is "the fulness of him who fills all in all" (Eph 1:23). It is Christ who opens and rules the church as the space of salvation.[25] The high ecclesiology in Ephesians cannot be understood apart from Christology. Being one body of Christ, the church is called to the one hope in Christ (cf. Eph 4:4–5). Christ himself gave various spiritual gifts for building up his body" (cf. 4:11–12). The goal of this edification is the unity of the knowledge of Christ and his fullness (cf. 4:13). Into Christ the body is to grow up; from him the whole body is joined, held together, equipped, working properly, and building itself up in love (cf. 4:15–16). Just as "Jesus Christ is not without his own," we can equally say that the church as his body is not without Christ.[26] As has been mentioned earlier, the bride metaphor needs to be related to a wider biblical theology. In Eph 5:29–30, the bride metaphor of the church is related to the body of Christ. Thus, here we can better understand the bride metaphor within the wider biblical theology.

3.6. Branches of the Vine

Without Christ the church as branches of the vine "can do nothing" (John 15:5). Prior to Schnelle, Minear had already written that here in this image "Christological reality is absolutely basic to the ecclesiological reality."[27] In the Old Testament, Israel as the people of God is portrayed as a vine which failed to bear fruit. When Christ said, "I am the true vine," the church should first humbly confess that he, not the church, is the true vine. Beasley-Murray rightly comments, "It seems likely therefore that the description of Jesus as the true Vine is primarily intended to contrast with the failure of the vine

24. Schnelle, *Theology of the New Testament*, 330.

25. Cf. Schnelle, *Einleitung in das Neue Testament*, 359.

26. Michael Welker, "Christian Theology: What Direction at the End of the Second Millennium?" in *The Future of Theology*, 79.

27. Minear, *Images of the Church*, 42.

Israel to fulfil its calling to be fruitful for God. That the Vine is Jesus, not the church, is intentional . . ."[28] The Johannine keyword *abide* (μένω) appears nine times in this discourse about the true vine (15:1–10).[29] If the church wants to be fruitful, she is to abide in Christ, the true vine. The abiding is reciprocal: not only is the church to abide in Christ, but Christ is also to abide in her. The abode of Christ and his words in the church guarantees her powerful prayer: "ask whatever you wish, and it will be done for you" (15:7). Yet this power and fruitfulness has a doxological goal: "By this my Father is glorified" (15:8). The vision of the Father's glory leads to an invitation to abiding in divine love (cf. 15:9). Abiding in divine love means the same as keeping divine commandments (15:10). Finally, all these things bring divine joy in the church (cf. 15:11).

Bearing much fruit is a proof of being Christ's disciples. What does John mean by the fruit? The reading of John 15:12–17 makes it clear that the fruit is no other than loving one another. It is not wrong to include "effective mission in bringing to Christ men and women in repentance and faith," yet the primary meaning of fruit here is reciprocal love.[30] In fact, the test of the true belief and right understanding of trinitarian perichoresis in the church is the demonstration of Christian mutual love. As the Father abides in the Son and the Son in the Father, so the disciples of Christ abide one in another through love. A fruitful church shows hospitality by inviting others to abide in her. The church is called to reduce the tension in the host–guest dualism by overcoming fear of aliens. In the light of Johannine Christology, Christ does not consider his disciples to be aliens but on the contrary, he invites them to abide in him and he in them (cf. John 15:4). Christ is both the host and the guest. The dualistic tension of host–guest is in this manner overcome in Christ. Ecclesiologically, the church must overcome this same dualistic tension as well: she is both the host and the guest. As a host, she invites people from all kinds to have table fellowship with her and with Christ. As a guest, she is to imitate Christ, who stands at the door and knocks, waiting patiently to be heard and for the door to be opened, to have table fellowship with all people (cf. Rev 3:20). An exclusive emphasis on the role of the church as a host can lead to triumphalist missiology. On the other side, an exclusive accent on the role of a guest will help serve the loss of the church's dignity.

28. Beasley-Murray, *John*, 272.

29. 3 in v. 4, 1 in v. 6, 2 in v. 7, 1 in v. 9, and 2 in v. 10.

30. Beasley-Murray, *John*, 273.

3.7. The Flock

The next metaphor for the church is that of the flock. The Christological image for this metaphor is Christ as the Good Shepherd. The flock metaphor calls for total dependency on Christ. Thus, the flock is to hear his voice (cf. John 10:3), to follow him and to know his voice (10:4), to flee from a stranger (10:5), to enter by him (10:9), and to be one flock with other sheep under one shepherd (10:16). The church as the flock lives under the promise of Christ, who gave his life for her. The church is to have life abundantly, i.e. the life of sacrifice in Christ (cf. 10:10–11). Carson contrasts Jesus as the Good Shepherd who gave life abundantly with the world's humanistic, political saviors such as Hitler, Stalin, Mao, and Pol Pot, who come only to destroy.[31] The church as the flock is to listen to and to enter by Jesus. Though the central point of the flock metaphor in Luke 12:32–34 is God's assurance of his unfailing care for his people,[32] the life of sacrifice in Christ is also implied: "Fear not, little flock, for it is your Father's good pleasure to give you the kingdom. Sell your possessions, and give to the needy. Provide yourselves with moneybags that do not grow old, with a treasure in the heavens that does not fail, where no thief approaches and no moth destroys." There is a close relation between the flock metaphor, God's assurance, and sacrificial life. Both John and Luke had economic aspect in mind when the first wrote about abundant life and the latter about treasure. John interweaves the flock metaphor in his seven "I am" sayings, while Luke connects this metaphor to his motif of reversal: the kingdom is given to the *little* flock. In Acts, the flock metaphor is related to the responsibility of the elders (cf. Acts 20:28).

Similarly, First Peter exhorts the elders to shepherd willingly the flock that belongs to God (cf. 1 Pet 5:1–2). They are not to be domineering but to be examples to the flock (cf. 5:3). Like John, Peter relates the flock metaphor to Christ "the Chief Shepherd" (5:4). None of the church elders is the chief shepherd; they are merely undershepherds appointed by Christ. This points us to the story of Peter's restoration. When Peter was being restored, he was appointed to feed and to tend the flock (cf. John 21:15–17). Peter in turn appointed fellow undershepherds to shepherd the flock. In this narrative, the shepherding of the church is not built upon a triumphant but upon

31. Carson, *Gospel according to John*, 385.

32. Bock cites Pss 23:1; 28:9; 74:1; 77:20; Isa 40:11; Jer 13:17; Zech 11:11; 13:7; Matt 9:36; Mark 6:34; 14:27; John 10:12; and Acts 20:28–29 to illumine the flock metaphor in the Old Testament. Bock, *Luke*, vol. 2, 1165.

a vulnerable elder who had been restored by Christ, so that the shepherding of the flock does not depend on human greatness but on Christ's suffering.[33] Coherently, shepherding the flock is not done by the elder's own resources but in the strength of Christ. In this regard Calvin wrote, "Let us also bear in mind the definition given of the word; for the flock of Christ cannot be fed except with pure doctrine, which is alone our spiritual food."[34] The implications of the church as the flock of God are that what is more needed in the church are examples, not domination. Since the church elders are undershepherds, they need to constantly refer the church to her chief Shepherd in their pastoral care. The flock is to listen to the voice of Christ. The church does not need great pastors; rather, she needs ordinary pastors who faithfully lead the flock to see the greatness of Christ and his pure doctrine. Vulnerable pastors will boast gladly of their weaknesses, so that the power of Christ may rest upon them (cf. 2 Cor 12:9).

3.8. The Light

The last metaphor for the church that we want to discuss is that of the light. While the light metaphor in the Scriptures is certainly very rich, we will only focus on the light metaphor related to the lampstand, which has a more specific range of meanings. Lampstand is not really a metaphor of the church. On the one hand, we read that the church was in danger of having the lampstand removed (cf. Rev 2:5), so that the lampstand was not the church herself. On the other, John the Presbyter wrote, "the seven lampstands are the seven churches" (Rev 1:20). John clearly thought that churches were meant to be lights of the world. This, lamentably, is not always the case. Stott warns, "No church has a secure and permanent place in the world. It is continuously on trial . . . Many churches all over the world today have ceased truly to exist. Their buildings remain intact, their ministers minister and their congregations congregate, but their lampstand has been removed."[35] In the Book of Revelation, the reason of the lampstand's removal is neither toil, nor endurance, nor sharp discernment of false apostles, but the abandonment of the first love (cf. Rev 2:2–4). Amid theological controversies about false teachings, what is at stake is not the inability to

---

33. Perhaps it is not a coincidence when First Peter refers to Peter as "a witness of the sufferings of Christ" (1 Pet 5:1).

34. Calvin, *Comm.* 1 Pet 5:2.

35. Stott, *What Christ Thinks*, 33.

test false teachings but the abandonment of love.[36] When a church becomes weary of loving, she no longer shines in the world; darkness will overpower her. Instead of becoming a foretaste of heaven, a church can become a foretaste of hell. Dostoyevsky powerfully writes that hell is the suffering of being unable to love. When Christ walks among the lampstands, churches keep their first love for him and do their first works. It is interesting to note that the lampstand is mentioned in the letter to the church in Ephesus, though each image could also be applied to other churches. Thus, the burning lampstand in the letter to Ephesus strongly relates to the love for Christ.

The love for Christ is the warmth of the propagation and maintenance of the gospel and truth of Christ.[37] *Doing the first works* means spreading the gospel of Christ with love and zeal. Christ himself is the gospel. A gospel-centered church will not abandon her first love for Christ; vice versa, a church that loves Christ will faithfully preach his gospel. In Rev 11, the two lampstands are linked with the two olive trees (v. 4), which may picture the church in her priestly and kingly roles.[38] If this interpretation is correct, then the two lampstands signify the church's proclamation of both forgiveness of sins (priestly function) and divine judgment (kingly function). Exercising kingly function without priestly function leads to cold orthodoxy; exercising priestly function without kingly function paves the way for secular humanism, for the biblical notions of God's forgiveness is not without God's righteousness.

In the Synoptics, the light metaphor is applied to Jesus and, derivatively, to his disciples. A lamp is not brought in to be put under a basket but on a (lamp)stand (cf. Mark 4:21; Luke 8:16; Matt 5:15). Mark and Luke placed this proverb-like saying after the Parable of the Sower and its purpose, so that we can relate the light metaphor to the fruitfulness of the Word (Mark 4:20; Luke 8:15). In this context, a lamp put on a lampstand means that God's revelation is not hidden but already revealed in Christ. Before the church can imitate Christ as the light to guide into the way of peace and for revelation (cf. Luke 1:79; 2:32), she should "take care then how you hear" (Luke 8:18). The church is to become the good soil, which holds the Word fast and bears fruit with patience (cf. Luke 8:15). Matthew placed the saying

---

36. Osborne comments that the Ephesians had "settled into a cold orthodoxy" thereby fulfilling Christ's prophecy that "The love of many will grow cold" (Matt 24:12). Osborne, *Revelation*, 115.

37. Cf. Poole, *Annotations upon the Holy Bible*, vol. 3, 953.

38. Cf. Osborne, *Revelation*, 422.

in a different context. The shining of the light is related to the disciple's good works (cf. Matt 5:16).

Various metaphors of the church, at least in this chapter, are relational images used to portray the church in her relation to Christ. Whether it is the metaphor of family, building, temple, bride, body, vine, flock, or light, they do not stand alone but are always thought in their relationship with Christ. They are references to Christ. Vice versa, a biblically sound Christology can help illumine the rich spectrum of meanings of the church metaphors.

4

The Government and Office-bearers
of the Church

4.1. Government

In the midst of the pressure from political, cultural, and economic policy, it should be restated that the "true church must be governed by the *spiritual* policy which our Lord hath taught us in His Word."[1] This spiritual policy implies that all church ministers "have equally the same power and authority," for Christ is "the only universal Bishop, and the only Head of the Church."[2] The Belgic Confession rejects the hierarchical Roman Catholic view of the office of ministry as had been taught by the Council of Trent. This rejection applies also to relations between churches: "No church will obtain primacy or dominion over other churches."[3] Similarly, Calvin pleaded that "administration of justice in the ancient church was not the function of an individual" but in the hands of the college of elders.[4] From a Reformed perspective, rejection of this collegial structure is a disbelief in the primacy of Christ, the head of the church.

The collegial structure helps to prevent anyone from representing Christ as the head of the church. However, this is not to say that because of

1. Belgic Confession, Art. 30; emphasis mine.

2. Belgic Confession, Art. 31.

3. Niesel, *Bekenntnisschriften und Kirchenordnungen*, 279, 1–2; quoted in Rohls, *Reformed Confessions*, 248.

4. Calvin, *Inst.* IV.11.6.

her spiritual nature, the church does not need any kind of visible government. Thus Calvin wrote that church laws are necessary for the right order yet they are not necessary for salvation.[5] There are criteria that can be used to distinguish between impious constitutions and legitimate church observances, which are decency, dignity, humanity, and moderation.[6] Regarding religious observances, Calvin allowed not only necessary change but also the abandonment of a certain law when it is deemed no longer required by the church as new circumstances arise.[7] Preserving church traditions which do not have any meaningful message to the contemporary world is untenable.

Rutherford vindicated the presbyterian model in the churches of Jerusalem, Corinth, Ephesus, and Antioch. The number of those who had received the Word in the early church was considerable (cf. Acts 4:4). Such a large number could not possibly meet in one place, let alone during the persecution of the church. Rutherford then concluded that those various churches in early Christianity were under one church government, which could not be congregational, because there were not only one congregation but many congregations that convened in divers places; therefore, their church government must have been presbyterial.[8] Although there were many congregations, the church government is one, because the seven deacons recorded in Acts 6 were office-bearers to all of them. Rutherford also used the Jerusalem Council (cf. Acts 15:1–21) as an evidence to support the presbyterian model, for in the council "the Elders doe presbyterially act for the removing of a *Church-scandall.*"[9]

The government of the church is a mediating act between God and his people yet the distinction between Christ and his church should always be maintained. In the words of Webster:

> The ministerial acts of Jesus Christ in the Spirit, by which he gathers, protects and preserves the church, are, properly speaking, incommunicable and non-representable . . . Whatever else we may wish to say about the mediating acts of the church's ministry, the barrier between Christ and the church must not be breached, for

5. Cf. Calvin, *Inst.* IV.10.27.

6. Cf. Calvin, *Inst.* IV.10.28.

7. Cf. Calvin, *Inst.* IV.10.32.

8. Cf. Rutherford, *Due Right of Presbyteries*, 438.

9. Rutherford, *Due Right of Presbyteries*, 452.

it is at this point that the principle of *solus Christus* finds its ecclesiological application.[10]

However, *solus Christus* does not exclude the idea that Christ wants to represent himself through church ministry. Webster cited Calvin on the reason for the need and the significance of church ministry.[11] For Calvin, God's government through the church and her ministers is an exercise in humility through showing teachableness toward God's ministers. Through his ministers, Christ "shows himself as though present by manifesting the power of his Spirit."[12]

The dialectic between the distinction (between Christ and the church) and Christ's presence through the church service should be preserved in the church. One-sided emphasis on the first will weaken the confidence and dignity of the church in her services. Conversely, one-sided emphasis on the latter will make the church into an arrogant and self-righteous institution that does not give glory to Christ. The servanthood of the church moves between her dignity as the body of Christ, "the fulness of him who fills all in all" (Eph 1:23) and her humble confession following John the Baptist that she is not the Christ (cf. John 1:20).

A sound ecclesiology should also preserve the dialectic between the community and the individual. The three classical models of the church government (the episcopal, the presbyterian, and the congregationalist) reflect the ecclesiological question whether the individual or the community comes first, which from the Reformed perspective needs not to be decided, for each presupposes and needs the other.[13]

The presbyterian model is a middle way between the episcopal and the congregationalist model, i.e., between the community and the individual. On the one hand, it does not give up the hierarchical structures. Calvin explained the necessity of teachers and ministers of the church in relation to the exercise of humility.[14] Hierarchical structures should not be con-

---

10. Webster, *Word and Church*, 199–200.

11. Cf. Calvin, *Inst.* IV.3.1, 2.

12. Calvin, *Inst.* IV.3.2.

13. If the community comes first, then we will have the episcopal model; if the individual comes first, then we will have the congregationalist model. The distinction between the hierarchical structures and the individual person also reflects a tension between covenant and election. Cf. Van der Kooi & Van den Brink, *Christian Dogmatics*, 583, 587.

14. Calvin, *Inst.* IV.3.1.

ceived as a way of exercising abusive power. Through a collegial govern-ment, the office-bearers of the church should acknowledge that no one is self-sufficient. Calvin went so far in his insistence on the significance of this ministry as to teach that those who abolished this kind of government were striving for the ruin of the church.[15] On the other hand, the presbyterian model focuses on personal faith and the responsibility of each member. Following Cyprian and providing scriptural testimony, Calvin rejected the election of the church minister by one person's authority and opted for the vote, "the consent and approval of the people."[16]

The common consent of the company of the faithful is also empha-sized in the *Ordonnances ecclésiastiques* of Geneva, though the calling of a church minister was elected by the pastors and then made known to the small council.[17] So that the local church would not be "defrauded of their liberty," they are permitted the right of objection.[18] While the *Ordonnances ecclésiastiques* permits only the right of objection, the Belgic Confession entrusts the legitimate election of ministers of the Word, elders, and dea-cons to the local church.[19] In the latter, the election of office-bearers of the church is less hierarchical than in Geneva. However, the Belgic Confession also admonishes that everyone in the local church should hold those office-bearers whom the local church elects in special esteem. Although there are slight differences between Belgic and Geneva, both affirm the importance of calling from a local church community. Without the role of the local church, it is hard to eliminate the absolute top-down ordination.

In Scotland, Presbyterian government was first introduced by John Knox and later strongly supported by Samuel Rutherford. After a lengthy discussion on the ordination and election of church ministers, Rutherford differentiated between ordinary and extraordinary cases. He concluded that in extraordinary cases of necessity, "election by the people only may stand for ordination, where there be no Pastors at all."[20] Two arguments are provided: first, God is not tied to succession of pastors; secondly, though ordinary means fails, the gift of the Spirit to certain men for the ministerial work where no pastor can be found is a sign of God's calling, so that no

---

15. Cf. Calvin, *Inst.* IV.3.2.
16. Calvin, *Inst.* IV.3.15.
17. Cf. Rohls, *Reformed Confessions*, 249.
18. Rohls, *Reformed Confessions*, 250.
19. Cf. Belgic Confession, Art. 31.
20. Rutherford, *Due Right of Presbyteries*, 187.

one should hinder election by the people. In such extraordinary cases, the calling of a church minister elected by the people is lawful.[21] However, in ordinary cases, "The established and settled order of calling of Pastors, is by succession of Pastors to Pastors, and Elders by Elders." Rutherford saw this rule as safe because it was the practice of the apostles (cf. Acts 1:15–16; 6:2–3; 14:23; 1 Cor 3:6; Titus 1:5).

In 1542, Calvin set up the Genevan Consistory as part of the implementation of his *Ordonnances ecclésiastiques*. The consistory consisted of pastors and twelve lay elders from the city councils. Their calling was to make sure that Genevans lived according to God's law in all aspects. The consistory exercised disciplinary actions which covered such matters as sexual immorality and marital issues, neighbor quarrels, tavern's regulation, cursing, unlawful lavishness, blasphemy, disrespecting the church, unorthodoxy, traces of Roman Catholic practices, gambling, swearing, etc.[22] From a modern perspective, the consistory's church discipline might sound too autocratic. What we can learn, however, is the seriousness in applying the evangelical faith in all areas of life. The problem of our contemporary church is no longer theological ignorance as in Calvin's time but the lack of integration between right doctrines and right practices, between knowledge and piety. The church should not lose the function of self-discipline, which is to take place in the custom of fraternal corrections.[23] The Consistory is to be differentiated from the so-called *Venerable Company*. The latter was a company of doctors and pastors who met quarterly for a purpose of mutual discipline.[24] The Consistory met weekly to discuss and exercise church discipline by baring Genevans who committed serious offenses such as blasphemy, drunkenness, adultery, etc. from the Lord's Supper.[25]

Church discipline is not the only goal of the spiritual government of the church according to Belgic Confession. Other goals include the preservation of true religion, the propagation of true doctrine, and the relief of the poor.[26] Far from abusing power, the church government deals lov-

21. Now in Scotland, where Presbyterian government was first established in a whole nation, the practice of the minister's election by each congregation seems to be the ordinary rule.

22. Cf. "Genevan Council Minutes and Public Announcements," in Maag, *Lifting Hearts*, 174–81.

23. Cf. the spirit of fraternal corrections in 2 Thess 3:15.

24. Cf. Lindberg, *European Reformations*, 248.

25. Cf. Lindberg, *European Reformations*, 249; see also Maag, *Lifting Hearts*, 68.

26. Cf. Belgic Confession, Art. 30.

ingly and mercifully with the needs of her children. Her government is a servant leadership. The church office-bearers are all Christ's servants. False office-bearers, like a false church, assign more authority to themselves than to God's Word, demanding others to submit to them rather than subjecting themselves to the yoke of Christ.[27] Christ's invitation to take his yoke means at the same time to learn from his gentleness and humility. Hence, a true church that submits herself to Christ's yoke exercises a gentle and humble government. On the contrary, a false church that does not submit to Christ creates her own uneasy yoke and will find restlessness. The true government of the church can be recognized by its distinguishing mark: namely, by her restfulness in Christ (not her youthfulness and restlessness).

4.2. Office-bearers

The office-bearers of the church are called apostles, prophets, teachers, evangelists, and shepherds (cf. 1 Cor 12:28; Eph 4:11). According to the Second Helvetic Confession, apostles ceased when churches had been established.[28] Similarly, prophets are no more because their words are "to be received and responded to" as the Words of God, whereas such direct prophetic revelations are no more, since we already have the whole counsel of God set down in Scripture.[29] Whether apostles, prophets, and evangelists already ceased or not depends on how we understand the term. The Second Helvetic Confession calls evangelists those, "who were the penmen of the history of the gospel, and were also preachers of the gospel of Christ," such as Timothy.[30] In this sense, evangelists are no more. Similarly, Calvin taught that the three offices of apostles, prophets, and evangelists were not established permanently, "but only for that time during which churches were to be erected where none existed before."[31] On the contrary, teachers and shepherds are not temporary but permanent offices.

---

27. Cf. Belgic Confession, Art. 29.

28. Second Helvetic Confession, XVIII.5.

29. Gaffin, *Perspectives on Pentecost*, 72; cf. WCF I.6.

30. Second Helvetic Confession, XVIII.5.

31. Calvin, *Inst.* IV.3.4; however, in his commentary on Ephesians, Calvin wrote that though these three offices were established temporarily, in certain cases "where religion has fallen into decay, and evangelists are raised up in an extraordinary manner, to restore the pure doctrine which had been lost." Calvin, *Comm.* Eph 4:11.

Scripture indeed argues for the cessation of the offices of apostles and prophets. On the foundation of the apostles and prophets, the household of God has been built (cf. Eph 2:19–20).[32] Though there is an aspect of continuation in that the Ephesians were expected to continue in the apostolic gospel and teaching, the offices of apostles and prophets have ceased, because the foundation of the church has been laid. This is supported by 1 Cor 3:10 when Paul wrote, "like a skilled master builder I laid ($\check{\epsilon}\theta\eta\varkappa\alpha$) a foundation, and someone else is building upon it."[33] The same principle can be said regarding the office of evangelists: evangelists are no more since the foundation of the early church has been laid. However, it can be understood differently. As an office-bearer who is appointed in mission and the erecting of churches, the office of evangelist can be said to have not ceased, when there are still a lot of areas where a single church has not yet been erected. As for teachers and shepherds, the New Testament clearly teaches that they belong to the office of elders.

Calvin taught four offices of the church, which are the pastors, the doctors, the elders, and the deacons.[34] Similarly, quoting Rom 12:7–8, Rutherford divided the church offices into four offices, which are the teacher or doctor, the pastor, the ruling elder, and the deacon.[35] We believe that the officers of the church in the New Testament should not be based on Rom 12:6–8, for here Paul merely listed different spiritual gifts.[36] More appropriate biblical passages for church offices are Phil 1:1 and 1 Tim 3:1–13. In both places only overseers/elders and deacons are mentioned. That in First Timothy, the two offices were in an undeveloped form is evident from the fact that Paul was more concerned with character than with established official duties (hence the list of qualifications for overseers and deacons in 3:1–13), so that this pastoral letter is closer to Paul's other letters than to Ignatius, who later developed the three offices hierarchical structure of bishop, elders, and deacons.[37] Thus, in this book we follow the two offices

32. The original ἐποικοδομηθέντες (having been built) is in aorist passive participle, which indicates something has already occurred.

33. The original ἔθηκα is in indicative aorist active.

34. Cf. Calvin, "Les Ordonnances ecclésiastiques de 1561," in Busch, Calvin-Studienausgabe, vol. 2, 238–59.

35. Cf. Rutherford, Due Right of Presbyteries, 157.

36. However, Ridderbos opines that the office is the charisma. Cf. Ridderbos, Paul, 444–45, 458–59.

37. Cf. Mounce, Pastoral Epistles, 154–55.

view instead of four. The offices of teacher and shepherd come under the office of elder.

4.2.1. Elder

The office of elder is responsible to teach and shepherd the flock of Christ. Peter exhorted his fellow elders to shepherd the flock of God (cf. 1 Pet 5:1-2). When he mentioned the chief Shepherd, Peter wanted to encourage fellow elders to be strong and faithful in overcoming many hindrances in their ministry. Calvin realistically wrote that elders "have often to do with ungrateful men, from whom they receive an unworthy reward; long and great labors are often in vain; Satan sometimes prevails in his wicked devices."[38] Against the temptation to give up and to be discouraged, Peter wrote about the promise of "the unfading crown of glory" (1 Pet 5:4). Elders are to pray and care for the sick (cf. Jas 5:14). They should work hard at preaching and teaching (1 Tim 5:17). Qualifications for their office can be found in 1 Tim 3:1-7 and Titus 1:5-9. Calvin highlighted certain qualifications in his commentary on Titus.

An elder or an overseer/bishop must not be arrogant or self-willed. An arrogant person only pleases himself, refuses to yield himself to others, and finally will become a fanatic.[39] This is one of the reasons why a church should be governed by a college of elders instead of one bishop. In his commentary on Titus, Calvin understood hospitality as docility, i.e. readiness and patience to learn.[40] He probably related this concept with what he believed to be "the chief gift in a bishop," which is holding firm to the trustworthy Word through the teaching office.[41] However, when commenting on First Timothy, Calvin understood hospitality literally:

> Besides, during the cruel persecution of the godly, many persons must have been constrained frequently to change their habitation; and therefore it was necessary that the houses of bishops should be a retreat for the exiles. In those times hard necessity compelled the churches to afford mutual aid, so that they gave lodgings to one another. Now, if the bishops had not pointed out the path to others in this department of duty, the greater part, following their

38. Calvin, *Comm.* 1 Pet 5:4.
39. Cf. Calvin, *Comm.* Titus 1:7.
40. Cf. Calvin, *Comm.* Titus 1:8.
41. Cf. Calvin, *Comm.* Titus 1:9.

example, would have neglected the exercise of humanity, and thus the poor fugitives would have been greatly discouraged.[42]

The importance of hospitality cannot be overemphasized in times of suffering and persecution of the church.

Gentle and not quarrelsome means knowing how to bear injuries gently, forgiving much, and not making himself be terrified by harsh severity.[43] A gentle bishop does not injure the flock by his excessive use of power; rather, he is ready to be hurt by the flock. Calvin clearly understood the office of bishop as a vulnerable shepherd in the love of Christ. Gentleness cannot be expected from a recent convert because gentleness is coherent with humility, not with haughtiness. Calvin followed Chrysostom when he interpreted the condemnation of the devil passively: by his pride a recent convert will fall into the same condemnation as the devil.[44] Finally, a good report by outsiders is important so that a bishop may not fall into disgrace by sinning "without any shame."[45]

4.2.1.1. Teacher

The office of teacher reflects the prophetic office of Christ. Christ was anointed to proclaim good news, the LORD's favor to the poor (cf. Isa 61:1). The teachers of the church continue this prophetic function by faithfully preaching the gospel of Christ. For Calvin, those, who are not content with the simplicity of the gospel, "detract from Christ's authority."[46] Christ became to the Corinthians wisdom from God (cf. 1 Cor 1:30), "in whom are hidden all the treasures of wisdom and knowledge" (Col 2:3), so that, except him, Paul decided to know nothing among the Corinthians (cf. 1 Cor 2:2). The teachers of the church should not fall into the temptation of presenting the gospel with lofty speech or human wisdom; rather, they are to deliver the gospel message "in demonstration of the Spirit and of power" (1 Cor 2:4). Paul's theology of the teaching office is trinitarian: the teachers of the church should seek the anointing of the Spirit, pointing solely to Christ crucified, and proclaiming the testimony of God.

---

42. Cf. Calvin, *Comm.* 1 Tim 3:2.
43. Cf. Calvin, *Comm.* 1 Tim 3:3.
44. Cf. Calvin, *Comm.* 1 Tim 3:6.
45. Calvin, *Comm.* 1 Tim 3:7.
46. Cf. Calvin, *Inst.* II.15.2.

Citing Tanner, Healy argues for a prophetic and practical function of an ecclesiological ethnography, which is opposed to what he calls "blueprint" ecclesiologies. Blueprint ecclesiologies make an effort to offer an idealized model of the church and dismiss the church's (concrete) sinfulness. Such an idealized model often ignores its particular context and temporary practicality. An ecclesiological ethnography, on the contrary, is "to open up our constructed identity to ongoing reassessment . . . by resisting the temptation to assume unified cultural totalities."[47] Every local community has its own failures and opportunities. The task of an ecclesiological ethnography is to discern those failures and opportunities. Such a theological approach will include the assessment of the church's ecclesial culture and other cultures as well. True ecclesial identity should be constructed and reconstructed in light of the truth of Christ instead of trying to preserve essential identity. Healy, thus, argues for dynamic self-criticism to expose the conflict, error, and sin of the concrete church. From the perspective of postmodern ethnography, we cannot speak of *the* culture as viewed by modern thinkers, for it undermines human responsibility to otherness and to cultural diversity. Ecclesiological ethnography creates a sensitivity to those who are marginalized by society.

Healy's approach is promising in that it provides theological realism instead of idealism. He is also right in his critique of a single supermodel elevated above all other models, for it fails to address the multifaceted nature of the church. However, his critique looks to weaken his own aims, for in order to identify the church's sinfulness one will need certain understandings of what the church ought to be.[48] He is also not clear about how Christ's lordship fit into his theological frame that encourages engagements with the wider secular culture.[49]

Affirming Healy's ethnography, we read in the gospel that Christ himself exercised constructive criticism of religion. Against the self-righteous lawyer who justified himself in his obedience to the Law, Jesus elevated a Samaritan (cf. Luke 10:25–37), a clearly marginalized other in Jewish society. The teaching office of the church is prophetic in that it considers the marginalized groups within society. It is not about confirming or reassuring one's own theological superiority, which often reflect the totalitarianizing by a specific group.

47. Healy, *Church, World and the Christian Life*, 175.
48. Cf. Stout, "Church, World and the Christian Life," 345.
49. Cf. Brown, "Church, World and the Christian Life," 983.

It should be noted, however, that considering the marginalized is not the goal of the teaching office. The goal is to proclaim the knowledge of God's righteousness in Christ, who invites all kinds of people to have table fellowship with him. Not only her mercy ministry, but the teaching ministry of the church should also serve and address all groups of people. Christ taught his disciples and the crowd, the poor and the rich, slaves and free, Jews and Gentiles; he offered table fellowship with both Simon the Pharisee and the sinful woman who anointed Jesus with the ointment (cf. Luke 7:36–50). The church's teachers shall not fail to address all people in their various callings: businessmen, lawyers, doctors, artists, politicians, reporters, educators, pastors et al. Christ taught different people context-sensitively. In the same way, Paul made himself a servant to all context-sensitively: to the Jews as a Jew, to the Gentiles as one outside the law, to the weak as a weak person (cf. 1 Cor 9:19–22). For the sake of the gospel, teachers of the church should become all things to all people in their teaching office.

The content of Paul's teaching is none other than the gospel of Christ (cf. 1 Cor 9:23). In his farewell to the elders of the church in Ephesus, Paul boldly testified that he "did not shrink from declaring to you the whole counsel of God" (Acts 20:27). The WCF understands this whole counsel of God as "all things necessary for his own glory, man's salvation, faith, and life."[50] It is the will of God the Father concerning mankind's salvation (cf. Gal 1:4), which called Paul to be an apostle of Christ (cf. 1 Cor 1:1). The will of God is the believer's sanctification (cf. 1 Thess 4:3). On the whole counsel of God, Matthew Henry comments:

> As he had preached to them the gospel pure, so he had preached it to them entire; he had gone over a body of divinity among them, that, having the truths of the gospel opened to them methodically from first to last in order, they might the better understand them.[51]

Teaching the whole counsel of God means to preach the pure gospel without adding or subtracting, nothing more and nothing less.

---

50. WCF I.6.

51. Henry, *Commentary on the Whole Bible*, 2157.

4.2.1.2. Shepherd

The office of shepherd, as the name suggests, concerns pastoral care in the church. When John portrayed Christ as the Good Shepherd, he related it to Christ's priestly office. In his gospel, John used repetitive priestly language in his Christology. Christ laid down his life for the sheep (John 10:11, 15, 17, 18). The Good Shepherd is none other than "the Lamb of God, who takes away the sin of the world" (John 1:29). Criticizing the corporate model of churches, Wagner rightly admonishes:

> In our love affair with all models contemporary, we have left be-
> hind the model that God himself both authorized and illustrated.
> The one model, the one role, that the Lord highlights for us in both
> Old and New Testament is that of shepherd.[52]

If we understand the office of shepherd in light of Christ's priestly office, church shepherds are to present themselves as living sacrifices of thankfulness to him and as faithful intercessors for the sheep.[53] The pastors are to keep the flock of the Lord.[54] A church pastor is first and foremost a good shepherd to Christ's flock, not an entrepreneur or a CEO of a corporation.

Similarly, the development of churches from the model of the state to civil associations placed certain pressures on pastors who had to be managers, for this managerial skill is strongly demanded to compete for church membership.[55] Welker observes that this in turn drives churches to constantly worry about their public role and presence, which is one of the reasons "why the 'aura of the pastoral office' seems to fade away."[56] Facing the emergent new polycentric world-view Welker proposes the rich and pluralistically textured structure of the biblical canon, the law traditions, the notions of the Spirit and the body of Christ, the texture of creation, and many other theological contents to counter the new world-view. As theologians, pastors should be equipped with God's given ability to discern the ever-changing world-view, to structurally map its constructive and

---

52. Wagner, *Escape from Church, Inc.*, 54.

53. Cf. HC 32.

54. Cf. Second Helvetic Confession, XVIII.5.

55. Cf. Welker, "Serving God," 84–85.

56. On the impacts of these developments on theology Welker emphasizes, "*While European churches and theologians often worried about the threat of the political power and its claims to loyalty, in nations without an official State Church the socio-political problem centers on questions of diversity and moral relativism.*" Welker, "Serving God," 82, 85.

destructive criticism against the previous fading world-view, and finally to context-sensitively challenge it with rich biblical notions.

According to Calvin, all pastors are teachers but not all teachers are pastors.[57] Pastors should be able to teach yet more than teaching is required from them. They are required to shepherd the flock of Christ with patient understanding of the flock, while at the same time guiding them to understand the will of God. As the Good Shepherd, Christ will guide his flock "to springs of living water" and "wipe away every tear from their eyes" (Rev 7:17). Though this verse is an eschatological promise, pastors are to anticipate this promise here and now as a foretaste of heavenly comfort and joy. A mature pastor shows sensitivity to the sorrow and grief of the flock rather than to his own wounds and disappointments. This is not to say that a pastor cannot present himself as a vulnerable human being. Vulnerable theology creates vulnerable office-bearers of the church, not stoic and triumphalist.[58] Vulnerable pastors are comforted by God in their affliction, so that they are enabled to comfort the flock with the comfort they receive from God (cf. 2 Cor 1:4).

4.2.2. Deacon(ess)

The following church office is the office of deacon/deaconess. The term διάκονος can be understood as servant in the general service of God (cf. 2 Cor 6:4; 11:23; Eph 6:21; Col 1:23; 1 Tim 4:6) or in an official role (cf. Phil 1:1; 1 Tim 3:8, 10, 12, 13). Deacons are distinguished from overseers/bishops. Their office is to render service (διαχονία). Their functions may have included assisting at the eucharist and collecting and administrating the offerings.[59] Qualifications for deacons can be found in 1 Tim 3:8–13. Though disputed in modern biblical scholarship, Calvin understood deacons with reference to Acts 6:3.[60] A sharp separation between teaching elders and deacons is not possible for the reason that deacons "must hold the mystery of the faith" (1 Tim 3:9). Holding the faith's mystery must include being

---

57. Cf. Calvin, *Comm.* Eph 4:11; see also *Inst.* IV.3.6.

58. On the difference between Christian forbearance and Stoic *apatheia*, see Calvin, *Inst.* III.8.9.

59. Cf. Roloff, *Kirche im Neuen Testament*, 143.

60. Cf. Mounce, *Pastoral Epistles*, 196; see Calvin, *Comm.* 1 Tim 3:8; note, however, Allison who viewed the origin of the office of deacon in Acts 6. Cf. Allison, *Sojourners*, 241.

well informed in the matter of right doctrine and sharing it in their pastoral ministry. Deacons must not be greedy but generous as it is required in their mercy ministry. Like bishops, deacons should be tested and their integrity proven. Some interpreters understand 1 Tim 3:11 as referring to deacon's wives, others to female deacons (deaconesses).[61] If the former interpretation is to be preferred, then deacon's wives are helpers to the ministry of their husbands. On the contrary, they will not be good helpers if they are not dignified and become slanderers. Though this is not to say that men are immune to the problem of slander, women are particularly vulnerable.[62] Deacons are to manage their own households well, so that they are able to manage the church as the household of God.

In his *Institutes* of 1536, Calvin already related the office of deacons to the mercy ministry. As has been mentioned above, he believed that the origin of this office was described in Acts 6. Calvin wrote, "This was the office of deacons: to attend to the care of the poor and minister to them; . . . For they are so called, as ministers."[63] He lamented the fact that in the medieval period, the tasks of the deacons had little to do with what was described in the New Testament. In his 1541 French *Institutes*, Calvin extended his writing with an introductory sentence: "Although the word *deacon* has a wide meaning, nevertheless scripture especially calls deacons those whom the church ordains to distribute the alms, as procurators and distributors of the public goods of the poor."[64] Here in this 1541 French edition, Calvin already distinguished between two kinds of deacon. Calvin was adapting to the already existing structures in Geneva. He might have found the two orders of deacons confirmed by the result of his study and commentary on Romans, which was published in 1540. In his commentary on Romans, Calvin explicitly distinguished between those "who presided in dispensing the public charities of the Church" and those "*who showed mercy*, . . . the widows, and other ministers, who were appointed to take care of the sick, according to the custom of the ancient Church."[65] Finally, while still criticizing the five other Roman Catholic sacraments, Calvin offered positive

61. Those who referred to deacon's wives include John Calvin, Matthew Henry, Herman Ridderbos, William Mounce, while those who referred to deaconesses include John Chrysostom, I. Howard Marshall, H. J. Holtzmann, J. Roloff, and Gene A. Getz; see the discussion in Mounce, *Pastoral Epistles*, 203–4.

62. Cf. Getz, *Elders and Leaders*, 107.

63. Calvin, [1536] *Institutes*, V.D.66, 171.

64. Calvin, [1541] *Institutes*, chap. 16, 612.

65. Calvin, *Comm.* Rom 12:8.

explanations on the office of deacon in the last edition of his *Institutes*.[66] The distinction between two kinds of deacon is maintained.[67]

Tuininga argues that Calvin's "two kingdoms" paradigm placed the care for the poor "as a distinct expression of the spiritual kingdom of Christ" that is represented in the church through the diaconate along with the civil authorities that represent the political kingdom through their office.[68] If his thesis is correct, then we can see the importance of the office of deacon in avoiding the removal of the care for the poor from the church by delegating it to social legislation. Mercy, along with justice and faithfulness, is one of the weightier matters of the law according to Christ (Matt 23:23). Without the mercy ministry exercised by deacons, the government of the church will lack an essential perspective, namely, that of the sorrows and sufferings of the people of God. The church is not called to govern in a political but in a spiritual manner, i.e. by her faithful proclamation of the secret counsel and will of God, by her sacrifice and continual intercession, and by the Word and Spirit of Christ.[69]

66. Cf. Calvin, *Institutes*, IV.19.32; IV.4.5; IV.5.5.

67. Calvin, *Institutes*, IV.3.9.

68. Tuininga, "God News for the Poor," 222.

69. Cf. HC 31–32.

5

The Ministries of the Church

THE CHURCH IS CALLED to various ministries which are related to her witness to Christ. There is a danger of being one-sided instead of having a multi-faceted ministry. An emphasis on merely one or two aspects does not do justice to Christ's abundant life. Thus, we refer to the kerygmatic, liturgical, pedagogical, communal, serving, pastoral, and testimonial aspects of the church's ministries.

5.1. The Proclaiming Church (κήρυγμα)

One of the most important ministries of the church is to proclaim the Word of God. A church receives the Word from the LORD and passes it on to the world. Christ has been anointed "to proclaim good news to the poor . . . to proclaim liberty to the captives . . ., to proclaim the year of the Lord's favor" (Luke 4:18–19). Luke understood the poor not in a political interpretation but as a generalization, i.e. as a reference to those who were more receptive to the proclamation of the gospel. On this verse, Bock comments, "it is the poor in general who sense their need in the greatest way . . . Their material deprivation often translates into spiritual sensitivity, humility, and responsiveness to God's message of hope."[1] This is not to say that there is no

---

1. Bock, *Luke,* vol. 1, 408. Similarly, Calvin commented, "But we are reminded, on the other hand, that we cannot enjoy those benefits which Christ bestows, in any other manner, than by being humbled under a deep conviction of our distresses, and by coming, as hungry souls, to seek him as our deliverer: for all who swell with pride, and do not groan under their *captivity,* nor are displeased with their *blindness,* lend a deaf ear to this prediction, and treat it with contempt." Calvin, *Comm.* Luke 4:18.

economic aspect to poverty in Luke. Compared to Matthew, Luke's understanding of poverty is not spiritualized (cf. Matt 5:3; Luke 6:20). The poor are those who are open and responsive to the proclamation of the gospel. Not everyone will respond positively to the church's proclamation; however, the poor and the captives are a great encouragement to the church.

The good news is the content of the church's proclamation. In Lukan writings, the verb εὐαγγελίζω (proclaim the good news) was used in Luke 2:10; 3:18; Acts 5:42; and 10:36. The first refers to the birth of Jesus the Savior; the second to the Messiah who will baptize with the Holy Spirit and fire with an appeal for repentance and the forgiveness of sins; the third to Jesus as the Messiah; and the fourth to peace by Jesus Christ, the LORD of all. The good news was never proclaimed in a vacuum but in the midst of poverty, captivity, blindness, and oppression. The failure to identify current poverty, captivity, etc. leads to an ineffective proclamation. If the church was to proclaim the liberating good news, she should be sensitive to the captivity of the world and sensitively address Christ's liberating deliverance. In Isaiah's ministry, the captivity was the exile; in John the Baptist's ministry, it was the fruitlessness and unrepentance of those who claimed to be Abraham's children (cf. Luke 3:8); in Jesus's ministry, it was the wrath and rejection of the religious people who worshipped in the synagogue, among others (cf. Luke 4:28).

A proclaiming church is at the same time a listening church. Without the sensitivity to listening to the Word of God, there is nothing to tell and to proclaim. In the Old Testament, false prophets did not proclaim God's truth. The LORD rebuked their human pleasing attitude: "They have healed the wound of my people lightly, saying, 'peace, peace,' when there is no peace" (Jer 6:14). On the contrary, true prophets only proclaim what they received from God, even if it costs them their safety. The study *Austritt oder Verbleib in der Kirche* (Leaving or Staying in the Church) written in 2012 by Michael Ebertz notes, "Young adults are hardly addressed by the traditional offers of the church and do not find them attractive."[2] Another study in 2014 by the Evangelical Church in Germany (EKD) lists "cannot do/start anything with faith" as one of the most strongly supported reasons

---

2. Christine Süß-Demuth, "Studie: Entscheidung für Kirchenaustritt ist langer Prozess" (Memento from 8. February 2013 in the *Internet Archive*), Pressemitteilung des Evangelischen Pressedienstes, 22 September 2012. Retrieved 11 February 2021, https://web.archive.org/web/20130208194909/http://www.epd.de/landesdienst/landesdienst-s%C3%BCdwest/studie-entscheidung-f%C3%BCr-kirchenaustritt-ist-langer-prozess-von-chr.

of leaving the church.[3] Without an awareness of her kerygmatic ministry, a church will lose her attractive power and radiance. Wendebourg rightly warns that poorly prepared sermons can be one of the reasons that a church will no longer radiate anything.[4]

5.2 The Worshiping Church (λειτουργία)

Concerning the church, the World Reformed Fellowship states, "The primary responsibility of the church is the worship of God."[5] The order of religious rites of this worship is called λειτουργία. The old formula *lex orandi est lex credendi* (the rule of praying is the rule of belief) makes us aware that the rule of faith (theological doctrine) was always shaped by the liturgical practices of the church.[6] Surely the worship practices of the church must be determined by doctrine. However, vice versa, the doctrine of the church is not based merely on scholastic reflections but also determined by the worship practices of the church.[7] One does not necessarily contrast liturgical practices over against the authority of Scripture as long as those practices are guided and inspired by Scripture.[8] The Scripture offers many patterns of worship that can be applied in our liturgy instead of one single pattern.[9] The riches of Scripture should be reflected in the rich liturgical practices. Only then will the people of God participate in the reenactments of God's salvific story. When Israel was commanded to celebrate the Passover in the promised land (cf. Exod 12:25–27), they were not asked to merely remember God's deed in the past, but to receive his salvific blessing in a fresh way.

In this sense, liturgy is by no means an empty order in Christian worship. Rather, it conveys Christ's benefits for the people of God each time we worship God. Calvin's Strasbourg's liturgy consisted of invocation and

---

3. "mit dem Glauben nichts anfangen zu können." EKD, "Engagement und Indifferenz," 90–91, March 2014, https://www.ekd.de/ekd_de/ds_doc/ekd_v_kmu2014.pdf.

4. Dorothea *Wendebourg im Gespräch mit Andreas Main*, "Kritik an Evangelischer Kirche in Deutschland," *Deutschlandfunk*, 13 June 2018, https://www.deutschlandfunk.de/kritik-an-evangelischer-kirche-in-deutschland-bei-uns-wird.886.de.html?dram:article_id=420178.

5. WRF Statement of Faith, VIII.3.

6. For historical discussion on the relation between *lex orandi* and *lex credendi*, see Wainright, *Doxology*, 224–27.

7. Cf. Chan, *Liturgical Theology*, 49.

8. Cf. Allison, *Sojourners and Strangers*, 38–39.

9. For possible patterns of worship, see Kristanto, *Place of Music*, 30–31.

call to worship, the confession of sins and words of absolution, Decalogue singing, reading of Scripture, psalm singing, prayer, sermon, collection of alms, intercessions and Lord's Prayer, Apostles' Creed singing, communion, *Nunc dimittis*, and benediction.[10] The invocation was taken from Ps 124:8. With this verse, Calvin wanted to proclaim that true worship confided in the help of God rather than in other worldly resources such as chariots and horses (cf. Ps 20:7).[11] The confession of sins reminds God's people that they are poor sinners before God's holy Majesty, condemning themselves with true repentance, forgiven by God, learning to struggle against all sins, and producing fruits of righteousness.[12] The Decalogue was put up in the Reformed churches to replace images of the Roman Catholic Church so that worshipers were rightly catechized.[13]

Reading of Scripture shall encourage worshipers to love and continuously meditate on the Word of God. In psalm singing, "we are certain that God puts the words in our mouths, as if he himself were singing in us to exalt his glory."[14] Prayer is for Calvin "the chief exercise of faith" that instructs believers "to recognize that whatever we need and whatever we lack is in God, and in our LORD Jesus Christ."[15] Preaching was for Calvin "something of a divine epiphany,"[16] in which the sheep hear unmistakably Christ's own voice.[17] Collection of alms was a response to Christ's teaching on the final judgment (cf. Matt 25:31–46). Calvin wrote:

10. Cf. Maxwell, *Outline of Christian Worship*, 114–15.

11. Cf. Calvin, *Comm.* Ps 124:8.

12. Cf. Calvin, "The Form of Prayers and Church Singing Together with the Way to Administer the Sacraments and Consecrate Marriage, Following the Practice of the Ancient Church (1542), in Maag, *Lifting Hearts*, 73–74.

13. Cf. Maag, *Lifting Hearts*, 30; a rural pastor wrote some reflections as advice to his successor: "I used to run these classes for about one hour and a half after the sermon. I used to set about it, every Sunday, by singing through the Ten Commandments with the men, and the women or girls, one table of the law at the beginning and the other at the end." Charles Perrot, "Managing a Country Parish: A Country Pastor's Advice to His Successor [1567]," in Maag, *Lifting Hearts*, 69.

14. Calvin, "Foreword to the Psalter (1545)," quoted in Maag, *Lifting Hearts*, 146–47.

15. Calvin, *Inst.* III.20.1.

16. Leith, "Calvin's Doctrine of the Proclamation of the Word," 31.

17. In his commentary on John, Calvin wrote, "Though he speaks here of ministers, yet, instead of wishing that they should be *heard*, he wishes that God should be *heard* speaking by them; for we must attend to the distinction which he has laid down, that he alone is a faithful *pastor* or *shepherd* of the Church, who conducts and governs his sheep by the direction of Christ." Calvin, *Comm.* John 10:4.

And (as Christian love [*charité*] requires) we testify this by holy offerings and gifts which are administered to Jesus Christ in His least ones, to those who are hungry, thirsty, naked, strangers, sick, or held in prison. For all who live in Christ, and have Him dwelling them, do voluntarily what the law commands them. And the latter commands that one not appear before God without an offering.[18]

Intercessions make us participate in Christ's priestly office. Believers embrace one another in prayer, being "related to the unity of the Head,"[19] while the Lord's Prayer helps believers to acknowledge God's boundless goodness and clemency.[20] All the clauses of the Apostles' Creed refer to— and are comprehended in Christ alone.[21] The special fruit of the Lord's Supper is union with Christ.[22] At the end of the Lord's Supper, *Nunc dimittis* was sung.[23] In his commentary, Calvin related Simeon's desire to depart in peace to his beholding of Christ as Israel's salvation. "More abundant materials of lasting peace" should be supplied to us, "who have the opportunity of beholding our salvation altogether completed in Christ."[24] Finally, more than just a pragmatic tradition of closing a service, benediction is an "efficacious testimony of God's grace . . . truly fulfilled in Christ, . . . who is the only sufficient surety of God's grace and blessing."[25]

Calvin also insisted that we may only worship God in ways that he has commanded. This doctrine is often called the "regulative principle of worship". The Belgic Confession teaches: "those who govern the churches . . . ought always to guard against deviating from what Christ, our only Master, has ordained for us. Therefore we reject all human innovations and all laws imposed on us, in our worship of God, which bind and force our consciences in any way. So we accept only what is proper to maintain harmony and unity and to keep all in obedience to God."[26] WCF understands what Christ has ordained for us as the acceptable way limited by God's own

---

18. Calvin, *La forme des prieres*, OS 2, 41–42; quoted in McKee, *John Calvin and the Diaconate*, 50.

19. Calvin, *Inst.* III.20.19.

20. Cf. Calvin, *Inst.* III.20.34.

21. Cf. Calvin, *Inst.* II.16.19.

22. Cf. Calvin, *Inst.* IV.17.2.

23. Cf. Maag, *Lifting Hearts*, 67.

24. Calvin, *Comm.* Luke 2:30.

25. Calvin, *Comm.* Num. 6:22, in *Harmony of the Law*, vol. 2.

26. Belgic Confession, Art. 32.

revealed will.[27] We conclude that for the Reformed tradition, the church liturgy should be shaped according to Christ alone.

5.3. The Teaching Church (διδασκαλία)

In the Great Commission, teaching is understood within the context of discipleship. Its goal is to observe all that Jesus had commanded his disciples. The scope of the church's teaching is thus the whole gospel of Jesus Christ. It is unfortunate that the Great Commission is sometimes reduced to a mere challenge to accept Jesus in one's own heart. Discipleship and teaching ministry are certainly much more than once in a life time personal decision to accept Jesus. In the Johannine writings, true discipleship is characterized by continuous abiding in Jesus, in his Word, and in his love (cf. John 6:56; 8:31; 15:4–7; 1 John 2:24, 27–28). A teaching church is not only preoccupied with intellectual information but with the power that transforms the Christian's affective lives. As in the ancient rhetorical theory, *docere* cannot be separated from *delectare* and *movere*.[28] Jesus's teaching was met with the astonishment of the crowds (cf. Matt 7:28). On the contrary, the scribes were teaching without authority.

Mere intellectual teaching is not the only problem of the church. On the other side, we may have an astonishing extent of emotion spawned in a church without it being related to a distinctive theological confession. Without objective contents, religious emotions cannot be distinguished from all other emotions. Thus, William James writes, "As concrete states of mind, made up of a feeling plus a specific sort of object, religious emotions of course are psychic entities distinguishable from other concrete emotions; but there is no ground of assuming a simply abstract 'religious emotion' to exist as a distinct elementary mental affection by itself, present in every religious experience without exception."[29] From a Christian perspective, James' teaching that religious affection is simply human natural emotion directed to a certain religious object cannot be approved. However, James is right when he says that without a specific sort of (religious) object, religious emotions are nothing but ordinary human emotions. It is the teaching of the church that shapes and makes religious emotions distinctively Christian.[30]

27. Cf. WCF XXI.1.

28. Cf. Cicero, *De Oratore*, 27.115.

29. James, *Varieties of Religious Experience*, 46.

30. In times of revival, the work of the Holy Spirit can produce various emotions and

The word διδασκαλία occurs eight times in First Timothy. Timothy was encouraged to be "trained in the words of the faith and of the good doctrine" (1 Tim 4:6), devote himself to teaching (cf. 4:13), keep a close watch on himself and the teaching (cf. 4:16). The term διδασκαλία appears in the Pastoral Epistles as proclamation of the gospel and ethical instruction for the Christian life.[31] Contrary to it are all kinds of lawlessness and vices (cf. 1 Tim 1:9–10). Yet, Mounce differentiates between the basic gospel message (words of the faith) and the doctrinal teaching (good doctrine) that comes out of it.[32] There could be a certain nuance between both, yet both entities are related. Sound teaching should come out of the gospel narrative. The teaching ministry of the church lies in its discernment between false teaching, i.e. teaching that does not come out of the gospel message and right teaching. Timothy was urged to fight against myths and endless genealogies (cf. 1 Tim 1:4); John struggled against Docetism (cf. 1 John 2:22; 2 John 7); Matthew against lawlessness (cf. Matt 7:21–23). Today, the church might have to fight against political correctness, hypocrisy, secularism, corporate business models, etc.

5.4. The Communing Church (κοινωνία)

κοινωνία is one of the keywords in the Lord's Supper. The cup of blessing is a participation in the blood of Christ; the bread a participation in the body of Christ (cf. 1 Cor 10:16). The church is sacramental in that she is a sign that refers to the true participation in Christ. The church is the body of Christ (cf. Eph 5:30), flesh of his flesh, bone of his bones.[33] The body of Christ had been broken so that the broken humanity might be gathered. The Lord's Supper is a proclamation of the death of Christ, who brings the members of his body into communion with himself. The participation in Christ is contrasted with idolatry, which is participation in demons (cf. 1 Cor 10:18–20), so that the church's witness of her fellowship with Christ

---

effects in the life of the believer. We need the ability to distinguish between spirits (cf. 1 Cor 12:10). Jonathan Edwards has provide a guide to discern true from false religious experience in the third part of his *Treatise Concrning Religious Affections*. Edwards, *Religious Affections*, 63–228.

31. Cf. Lohfink, "Paulinische Theologie in den Pastoralbriefen," in Kertelge, ed., *Paulus*, 99.

32. Cf. Mounce, *Pastoral Epistles*, 249.

33. Calvin, *Comm.* 1 Cor 10:16.

is at the same time a witness of her true worship. Christian fellowship is a fellowship of true worship. κοινωνία and λειτουργία are inseparably linked.

Because the church's fellowship is a fellowship with Christ, it includes sharing in his sufferings (cf. Phil 3:10; 1 Pet 4:13) and his glory (cf. 1 Pet 5:1). This fellowship may be the result of the church's faithful commitment to the gospel narrative. It could come as a fiery trial to test believers when they are insulted for Christ's name (cf. 1 Pet 4:14). Suffering can never be the goal of the church; yet, it always accompanies Christ's faithful church. The church in Smyrna was known for her tribulation and poverty. The church in Philadelphia was known for her patient endurance. As the witness of Christ's suffering, the church will also be a partaker in Christ's future glory. An implication of this eschatological hope is that the church's elders should shepherd the flock of God willingly, eagerly, and by being examples (cf. 1 Pet 5:2–3).

The fellowship of the believers is a fellowship in the apostles' teaching and in prayer (cf. Acts 2:42). Here, κοινωνία and διδασκαλία are inseparably joined. The early church is characterized by the generosity and hospitality of her members. She was a fellowship of giving and receiving to and from one another. She stood in opposition to the deed of Ananias and Sapphira, or to what Peter called exercising oversight "for shameful gain" (1 Pet 5:2). The fellowship in Christ's sufferings means a fellowship in the sufferings of fellow Christians. John called himself a "partner" (συγκοινωνός) in the tribulation (Rev 1:9). Similarly, Paul wrote that there was togetherness in the suffering of one member (cf. 1 Cor 12:26). To Philemon Paul wrote and asked him to consider Paul his "partner" (κοινωνός), so that he might receive Onesimus (Phlm 17). κοινωνία includes even a social dimension that could break through the ancient social structure of the house by granting a new social status to the underprivileged.[34]

Still in relation to suffering, the Corinthians not only shared in Paul's and Timothy's sufferings, but also in their comfort (cf. 2 Cor 1:7). The church does not prepare and plan sufferings for the people of God; yet a healthy church prepares her members to share in other's sufferings. The goal of fellowship in other's sufferings is the sharing in the comfort of Christ, who leads believers to the Father, God of all comfort. A Christian is not comforted individually but communally in the church. The Philippians also shared Paul's trouble by entering partnership with Paul in giving and receiving (cf. Phil 4:14–15). Paul could say that he could do all things

---

34. Cf. Schnelle, *Einleitung in das Neue Testament*, 171.

through Christ who strengthened him, not least through the fellowship of the church in Philippi, which shared in Paul's trouble. Sharing in other's burden and trouble leads to contentment in Christ.

In the beginning of the Epistle, Paul thanked God because of the Philippian's partnership in the gospel (Phil 1:5). There should be a fellowship of evangelizing work in the church. Those who faithfully proclaim the gospel will have fellowship with fellow evangelizing brothers and sisters. Such fellowship gives strong eschatological hope that God will bring to completion the good work that he began (cf. 1:6). Here, again, we see that fellowship in the gospel is not reduced to merely calling unbelievers to accept Jesus in their hearts; it rather means a continuous fellowship in hoping, witnessing, and participating in other's good work until its completion. Sharing in the spiritual blessings of others ought to evoke a sense of responsibility to serve them in material needs (cf. Gal 6:6; Rom 12:13; 15:26–27; 2 Cor 8:4; 9:13).

5.5. Serving Church (διακονία)

Serving others in their material needs is what the Scripture calls *diakonia*. It can be generally translated as service or ministry. If the church's rejection of docetic Christology is sincere and not merely rhetorical, she should participate in concrete deeds of mercy for the poor and the needy. In the early church, the twelve viewed diakonia so highly that they summoned the disciples to pick out seven men full of the Spirit appointed to this ministry. When "the word of God continued to increase, and the number of the disciples multiplied greatly" (Acts 6:7), it was not without the mercy ministry of the church. A church that neglects diakonia as an insignificant priority in her ministries will hardly see the increase of the Word of God and the multiplication of disciples. Discipleship always includes attending to the physical needs of the body of Christ, though not exclusively. It is true that diakonia can be used with regard to the spiritual needs as well (cf. Acts 6:4; 20:24; 21:19); yet the church can never exclude its physical aspect.

Diakonia points to and witnesses to the generosity of Christ, the Head of the church. The church is not invited to accumulate wealth for herself, for such endeavor cannot be based on the life of Christ. The diaconal charisma of the church cannot be separated from and should be strengthened through the kerygmatic and teaching ministry of the church. This prophetic-ethical dimension belongs to the following of Christ within diakonia.[35]

---

35. Cf. Welker, "Kirche und Diakonie in säkularen Kontexten," 39.

The Messiah was prophesied by Isaiah to bring justice, protect the weak, and bring universal knowledge of God; this task is now entrusted to the church.[36] There is no true knowledge of God without mercy ministry and vice versa. Kerygmatic without diaconal ministry makes a church into a mere institution of propaganda. Such churches do not believe that "it is more blessed to give than to receive." On the other side, diaconal without kerygmatic ministry will transform a church into a mere social foundation. Christ did not only serve the poor but also came to "bring good news" to them (Isa 61:1).

Similarly, diakonia as ministerial protection of the weak is insepara-bly linked to bringing justice. Whereas traditionally, justice is thought of as the opposition to injustice, in contemporary theories of justice, it can also be contrasted with generosity or mercy. Thus, Rawls writes, "The least advantaged are not, if all goes well, the unfortunate and unlucky—objects of our charity and compassion, much less our pity—but those to whom reciprocity is owed as a matter of basic justice."[37] There is a certain truth in Rawls's theory of justice in that the poor and the needy are in many cases victims of systemic injustice in the world. However, mercy ministry is not identical with and cannot be replaced by the fight for basic justice. Jesus said, "you always have the poor with you, and whenever you want, you can do good for them" (Mark 14:7). No matter how serious the church fight against injustice, there will always be the poor around us. Through diaconal ministry, the church learns to imitate and follow the footsteps of Christ.

5.6. The Counselling Church (ποιμήνία)

In the New Testament, the counselling ministry is entrusted to the elders as pastors, to those who receive the gift of exhortation (cf. Rom 12:8), and finally to all believers (cf. 1 Thess 5:14; Heb 3:13). The elders of the church are to pay careful attention to all the flock, to care for the church of God (cf. Acts 20:28), to pray for the sick (cf. Jas 5:14), and to shepherd the flock of God willingly (cf. 1 Pet 5:1–2). Believers are to exhort one an-other, that none may be hardened by sin (cf. Heb 3:13). Pastoral ministry can appear in terms such as παράκλησις, νουθετεῖν, and καταρτίζειν, which

---

36. For Welker, Calvin's insights that Christ pours out his Spirit on his own and gives the church a share in his divine powers are Christologically groundbreaking. Cf. Calvin, *Inst.* II.15.

37. Rawls, *Justice as Fairness*, 139.

can be expressed as *exhortation, encouragement, admonition,* and *comfort in the New Testament.*[38] In his epistles, Paul listed the gift of exhortation (παράκλησις) along with other gifts of grace such as the ministry of prophecy, serving (διακονία), teaching (διδασκαλία), and mercy (cf. Rom 12:6–8; 1 Tim 4:13).

Encouragement (παράκλησις) is also linked to participation (κοινωνία) in the Spirit, both of which will lead to the unity of the church (cf. Phil 2:1–2; 1 Cor 1:10). The church should direct her counselling ministry to the idle, the fainthearted, and the weak (cf. 1 Thess 5:14). Paul applied an eclectic method when he urged the Thessalonians to admonish the idle, encourage the fainthearted, help the weak, and be patient with them all. The eclectic method is a combination of directive and non-directive method. Whereas in the directive method, the counsellor uses the Word of God to admonish and challenge the counselee, in the non-directive method, the counsellor guides, encourage, and empathize with the counselee and his/her situation in light of the Word of God. In Luke 10:34–35; Acts 20:31; Rom 12:13; and Titus 2:15, we find both directive and non-directive method. There is a *kairos* for every matter, a time to apply the directive, and a time to apply the non-directive method.

Those who need to be healed and taken care of (cf. Luke 10:34–35), to be provided hospitality (cf. Rom 12:13), and to be exhorted and rebuked (cf. Titus 2:15) are those whom the church may counsel.[39] However, not only those people but everyone in the church in Ephesus was faithfully admonished (νουθετεῖν) by Paul for three years (cf. Acts 20:31). Everyone in the church in Colossae was warned (νουθετεῖν) and taught with the goal of maturity in Christ (cf. Col 1:28). To present everyone mature is to supply (καταρτίζειν) what is lacking in faith (cf. 1 Thess 3:10). Paul and Timothy were able to comfort those who were in affliction with the comfort (παράκλησις) which they received from God (cf. 2 Cor 1:4).

Pastoral ministers of the church are not only comforters; they, too, need to be comforted. Those who place themselves above the flock tend to fall victim to pride. Nash speaks of what he calls "Caesar's Syndrome," which makes a minister think: "I know more about God's truth and God's will than my people. Moreover, I am more spiritual than they . . . Given my greater proximity to God, it must follow that any member of my

---

38. Cf. Möller, *Seelsorglich predigen*; see also Godzik, ed., *Sterbebegleitung*, 30.

39. Cf. Müller, "Seelsorge II. Historisch-theologisch," in Kasper, ed., *Lexikon für Theologie*, col. 385.

congregation who is properly submissive to God will also be submissive to me."[40] Instead of becoming a faithful overseer by being examples to the flock, such minister will be domineering over those in their charge (cf. 1 Pet 5:3). Not only her ministers but also the church herself should minister the flock as the vulnerable yet beloved bride of Christ. The church is not without the need for God's comfort. God's consolation in the care of souls can take form in "the mutual conversation and consolation of brothers and sisters," wrote Luther.[41] For Anderson, Luther understood the church as a community that not only worships together publicly, but also that reclaims the priesthood of all believers as shepherds of the soul.[42]

5.7. Witnessing Church (μαρτυρία)

Finally, the church according to Christ is a church that witnesses about Christ. As a verb, μαρτυρέω means speaking well of someone (cf. Luke 4:22; Acts 10:22), someone who is of good repute or well-spoken of (cf. Acts 6:3; 16:2; 22:12; Col 4:13; 3; 1 Tim 5:10; John 6, 12). John the Baptist is a witness model for the church. He was a witness who bore witness about Christ, the light (cf. John 1:7). The setting in life of witness or testimony is in the courtroom.[43] Like John the Baptist, the church is called to witness about the righteousness of Christ, who is being accused by the unbelieving world. The first chapter of the Gospel of John already anticipates Christ's crucifixion. First, John the Baptist was a witness about the accused and persecuted Christ. Later in his life, he himself would be in the place of the accused. The same principle holds true for Jesus's disciples and the life of the church as Christ's witness. The church that witnesses about Christ's suffering will suffer on Christ's account (cf. Matt 5:11).[44] However, John's disciples bore him witness, that he was not the Christ (cf. John 3:28). Following John, the church should also witness that she is not Christ. The church merely walks in his footsteps.

---

40. Nash, "Shepherding Overseers," 3.

41. Luther, "Smalcald Articles," 319.

42. Anderson, "Shepherding Souls," 54.

43. See Carson, *Gospel according to John*, 120.

44. In Revelation, authentic witnesses of Christ are known by the suffering for the sake of their testimony. Cf. Rev 2:13; 6:9; 11:7; 12:11; 17:6; 19:10; 20:4; cf. Schnelle, *Theology of the New Testament*, 764.

The calling to witness always involves polemics, for witness about the truth cannot be separated from rebuke to the unrepentant. John the Baptist was locked up in prison by Herod, whom John reproved for marrying Herodias and for all his evil deeds (cf. Luke 3:19–20). Jesus was crucified because he never failed to fight against corrupted political, economic, social, cultural, and religious ideologies during his life. Silence against injustice and demonic ideologies is the failure to witness. In his commentary on Matthew, Calvin wrote:

> In other words, he [Christ] intends that the profession of his name shall be set in opposition to false religions: and as it is a revolting matter, he enjoins the testimony which we must bear, that the faith of each person may not remain concealed in the heart, but may be openly professed before men.[45]

To the women detained in prison in Paris, Calvin wrote about faithful martyrs that "there is no preaching of such efficacy as the fortitude and perseverance which they possess in confessing the name of Christ."[46] Preaching is usually understood as a form of verbal witnessing, whereas witnessing is believed to have a wider meaning. However, for Calvin, faithful witnessing can function as a powerful preaching, for it efficaciously present Christ whom one believes in as one's way of life. From preaching to witnessing, the church should point to the person and the works of Christ in her ministries.

---

45. Calvin, *Comm. Matt* 10:32.
46. Calvin, *Writings on Pastoral Piety*, 332.

6

The Sacraments

REFORMED THEOLOGY OF THE Holy Sacraments is a *via media* between highly magical sacramentalism on the one side and rationalistic empty symbolism on the other. It explains the relation between signs and things signified as unconfused yet unseparated. The signs are distinct from the things signified yet both are in union. Thus, the Heidelberg Catechism distinguishes between the outward washing with water in Baptism (sign) and the cleansing by Christ's blood and the Spirit (things signified).[1] They are not to be confused. Yet, at the same time, the sign should not be separated from the things signified. The HC formulates this inseparable union in the promise of Christ that, "as surely as water washes away the dirt from the body, so certainly his blood and his Spirit wash away my soul's impurity, that is, all my sins."[2] To be distinguished does not mean to be separated; to be in union does not mean to be confused.

Sacrament has a double meaning: the outward and the inward, physically and spiritually, visible and invisible. Just like there are the dangers of the ancient heresies in the broader scope of ecclesiology, there are also the heretical dangers with regard to the theology of sacrament. A false sacramentology separates the signs from the things signified or confuses the signs with the things signified. Those who equate physical washing with spiritual washing or bread with the body of Christ do not safeguard the distinction between the sign and the thing signified. The visible is not to

1. Cf. HC 72.

2. HC 69; all translations of the HC are taken from Bierma, *Theology of the Heidelberg Catechism*.

be confused with the invisible. Yet, distinguished does not mean separated. Thus, the Second Helvetic Confession speaks of the sacramental union in that "the signs and the things signified are sacramentally joined together."[3]

6.1. Holy Baptism

Though Holy Baptism is to solemnly admit one into the visible church, it is also a sign of the ingrafting of the baptized into Christ.[4] The visible and the invisible aspect are not separated for they reflect Christ's hypostatic union. Baptism is a token of the believer's union with Christ.[5] For Paul, being baptized into Christ means being baptized into death (cf. Rom 6:3). Baptism is a sign of being buried with Christ into death (cf. Rom 6:4), so that believers might mortify sin through the power of the Holy Spirit. The central notion of baptismal theology in Romans is union with Christ: "if we have been united with him in a death like his, we shall certainly be united with him in a resurrection like his" (Rom 6:5).[6] For Paul, the crucifixion of the old self is an event happened already in the past; the believer's presence is characterized by a new life in Christ. Baptism confers the identity of the new self in Christ.

The Second Helvetic Confession views baptism as a separation from all strange religions and consecration to newness of life. This newness is no other than constant mortification of the flesh and spiritual war, for those who have been baptized are "enlisted in the holy military service of Christ."[7] The military dimension of baptism is characteristic in the Zwinglian tradition. This helps the church not to fall into complacency and spiritual lethargy. Since through baptism believers are ingrafted into the body of Christ, they also share in Christ's anointing, especially with regard to his kingly office.[8]

3. Second Helvetic Confession, XIX.

4. Cf. WCF XXVIII.1.

5. Cf. Calvin, *Inst.* IV.15.1.

6. Schnelle writes, "Baptism is the place of effective and full participation in the Christ event." Schnelle, *Apostle Paul*, 331.

7. Second Helvetic Confession, XX.

8. For the HC, in the sharing in Christ's anointing, a Christian is anointed "to strive with a free conscience against sin and the devil in this life, and afterward to reign with Christ over all creation for eternity." HC 32.

In the ingrafting into Christ, said Calvin, believers not only derive nourishment from Christ but also pass from sinful nature to Christ's holy nature.[9] A change of nature takes place in baptism. Believers would no longer be enslaved to sin but set free (Rom 6:7). The new given nature creates submission, to present the bodily members as instruments for righteousness (Rom 6:13). Calvin too noticed the military dimension in this verse, thus highlighting the idea of a change of ruler from the reign of sin to the reign of Christ.[10] Similarly, Welker also emphasizes this change of rule in baptism.[11] For him, the change is connected to the "fulfilment of all righteousness" (cf. Matt 3:15).[12] This fulfilment manifests itself both in God's gracious turning to humans and among humans in the relationships of love and forgiveness. Echoing Calvin and Welker, we can say that baptism not only serves as the initial rite into the visible church but also as the believer's oath of allegiance to Christ, who has fulfilled all righteousness in mercy and love.

In that sense, baptism is not merely a personal, let alone an individual matter. Just as the understanding of the sign in a Reformed theology of the sacrament is not an empty symbolism, so we have to understand baptism as a witness to *both* the spiritual cleansing by the blood and Spirit of Christ *and* the ingrafting into Christ. With regard to the former, the baptized receives the forgiveness of sins in Christ; with regard to the latter, the visible church is once again called to reflect Christ's kingly office in fulfilling all righteousness. Righteousness manifests itself not only in love relationships among members of the church but also in the distribution of power in church government. This is not to say that the church government should be egalitarian but that the administration of justice in the church should not be the function of an individual.[13] Baptism points to the righteous kingdom and reign of Christ. It is a polemical statement against abusive human rulership. The church should consider not only the Trinitarian

---

9. Cf. Calvin, *Comm.* Rom 6:5.

10. Cf. Calvin, *Comm.* Rom 6:13.

11. Welker points out that Jesus's baptism takes provocation to extremes. The medium of encounter with God is no longer the high priest, the temple, the Yom-Kippur, and the ritual sacrifice; the true medium is Jesus Christ. A change of rule from Jewish religious authorities to Jesus took place in his baptism. Cf. Welker, *God the Revealed*, 285–86.

12. Welker, "Die Taufe," in *Geöffnet*, ed. Schwier, 148.

13. Cf. Calvin, *Inst.* IV.11.6.

formula in the Great Commission but also Jesus's saying that all authority in heaven and on earth had been given to him.

Another communal aspect of baptism in the Reformed tradition can be found in the Reformed teaching of infant baptism. Thus, in the HC the reason for infant baptism is because both infants and adults "are included in God's covenant and people" and "promised deliverance from sin through Christ's blood and the Holy Spirit."[14] Through this sign of covenant, they must be distinguished from the children of unbelievers. In this context, baptism confers communal identity. To quote Minear once again, being one people of God, the baptized receives the "story" and the "common character" of the family of God.[15] Through baptism, the baptized is given a Christian narrative to live.

Baptism is also a means of assurance. The HC starts the treatment of baptism with the question: "How does holy baptism remind and *assure* you that Christ's one sacrifice on the cross benefits you personally?"[16] Venema rightly laments that in many Reformed churches this aspect of assurance is ironically belittled.[17] The over suspicion upon the danger of idolatrous sacramentalism has paved the way for a low view of sacrament in Reformed theology. The outward washing is certainly to be distinguished from the spiritual washing; yet they cannot be separated. It is not without good reason that in Titus baptism is called "the washing of regeneration" (3:5) because the outward washing should not be disconnected from the spiritual regeneration.[18] Calvin aptly commented:

> The efficacy and use of the sacraments will be properly understood by him who shall connect the sign and the thing signified, in such a manner as not to make the sign unmeaning and inefficacious, and who nevertheless shall not, for the sake of adorning the sign, take away from the Holy Spirit what belongs to him.[19]

The distinction *and* union between the thing and thing signified should be perceived from the doctrine of Christ's two natures. Reformed theology of

---

14. HC 74.

15. Minear, *Images of the Church*, 166.

16. HC 69.

17. Cf. Venema, "Sacraments and Baptism," 85–86.

18. Almost all modern writers hold that the creed in this verse refers to baptism with a few exceptions including Norbie, Fee, and Mounce; cf. Mounce, *Pastoral Epistles*, 448. Historically, Calvin and the HC believed that the verse referred to baptism.

19. Calvin, *Comm.* Titus 3:5.

the sign does not have to lead to a low view of sacraments. On the contrary, Christ instituted the sign in order to assure us of the spiritual reality, which is given to us and of which we partake.

Welker rightly suggests that just as the celebration of the Lord's Supper is based on Jesus's institution of the sacrament, Christian baptism is also based on the baptism of Jesus.[20] In addition to the change of rule to the kingdom of God and its claim, the revelation of true identity, meaningful relationship, and the direction of the course of life also took place in Jesus's baptism. Jesus is the Father's beloved Son, with whom the Father is well pleased. In Jesus, our identity as children of God is given from above through baptism. We do not search for identity, let alone obtain it through achievement, performance, or productivity.[21] There is a certain beauty in infant baptism in this context: infants are not yet able to perform anything and they are already given a new identity as children of God. The gift of identity stands in contrast with the tower of Babel where human beings want to "make a name" for themselves. Through baptism, the church witnesses that her identity is not acquired through her performance but received from above. A healthy church does not struggle for identity. Secondly, Jesus's baptism reveals the love relationship between the Father and the Son. Jesus is the beloved Son of the Father. The church is the beloved bride of Christ. Love relationships are contrasted with both oppressive and contractual relations and to be witnessed in the midst of them.

Oppressive relations do not give space for others, whereas contractual relations, though seemingly egalitarian, do not have any objective bond and goal. Oppressive relations are against the baptism narrative. Thus, John the Baptist challenged the crowd that came to be baptized by him to bear fruits in keeping with repentance, to share clothing and food, to not collect and extort money beyond authorization, by threats or false accusation (cf. Luke 3:8, 11, 13–14). Repentance from oppressive relations is required in baptism, for through baptism believers enter into love relations. However, love relations are not contractual relations. Love relations are built upon the covenant between God and his people. According to the HC, baptism is a sign of the covenant.[22] In the covenant that God made between him

---

20. Cf. Matt 3:13–17; Mark 1:9–11; Luke 3:21–22; see Welker, *Gottes Offenbarung*, 283.

21. In the temptation, Jesus was precisely tempted by the devil to prove his identity through what he could perform and achieve.

22. Cf. HC 74.

and Abram, God promised to be his God and his offspring's, while Abram should walk before God and be blameless (cf. Gen. 17:1, 7). In a contractual relation, when both parties can no longer reach an agreement, relation can be broken or terminated. Faithfulness is not required in a contractual relation, for there is no objective goal but only subjective preference and liking. In the covenantal love relation, which is signified through baptism, on the contrary, the baptized enter into a new family, the family of God, in which love and faithfulness reign.

Lastly, Jesus's baptism also reveals that human search for pleasure is misguided. The highest enjoyment is received when God is pleased. There is a danger when a church becomes like the Jewish religious authorities in the time of Jesus. Those authorities failed to please God. The church can only please God the Father through the Son, with whom the Father is well pleased. What does this mean? It means that no church should claim that she pleases God for he, with whom God is pleased, is his only beloved Son. The church can only please God in the derivative sense, when she partakes of the anointing in Jesus's baptism. It is true that believers please God in believing in God (cf. Heb 11:5), in sharing the gospel (cf. 1 Thess 2:4, 8), in presenting their bodies as a living sacrifice (cf. Rom 12:1), in serving Christ (cf. Rom 14:18), in discerning between light and darkness (cf. Eph 5:8–11), in walking in a manner worthy of God (cf. Col 1:10), in obeying their parents (cf. Col 3:20), in praying and thanksgiving for all people (cf. 1 Tim 2:3), and in keeping his commandments (cf. 1 John 3:22), yet all of these depend on the believer's participation in Christ by the Spirit. There is an allusion to Isa 42:1 in the voice of the Father.[23] In Isaiah, the servant, in whom God's soul delights, is God's chosen.[24] The anointing of the servant is tightly related to the kingly function: "he will bring forth justice to the nations" (Isa 42:1). It is thus not a coincidence when Matthew wrote that the reason for Jesus's baptism was "to fulfill all righteousness" (Matt 3:15). The church is called to witness the story of the "better righteousness" made possible through the anointing of the Son of God in his baptism.[25] The righteousness of the church is to exceed that of the scribes and Pharisees in the sense that the church is to teach the radicalization (not the relaxation)

23. Cf. Hagner, Matthew 1–13, 59.

24. Carson rightly comments that the reinforcement of the aorist tense may suggest a pretemporal election of Christ. Cf. Carson, "Matthew," 109.

25. Cf. Matt 5:20; for the explanation of the better righteousness, see Schnelle, Theology of the New Testament, 446.

of the Torah's commandments (cf. Matt 5:19). The problem of many evangelical churches today is that, in the name of the gospel, the preaching of the law has frequently become suspect to legalism. What we have here is actually a cheap grace gospel. Baptism is a pledge of God's grace to us; at the same time it is also a pledge of the baptized to observe all of Jesus's commandments (cf. Matt 28:20).

In Matthew's Great Commission, baptism is inseparably related to discipleship. Baptism encourages sending and mission. When Christians witness the sacrament of baptism in the church, our hearts should be filled with the zeal of reaching out to all nations. Just as the Lord's Supper is a commemoration of the salvific death of Christ, baptism is a testimony that Christ has been given all authority over all nations. It is a witness to Christ's supreme authority not merely in a local church but in heaven and on earth. Baptism is not a static contemplative sacrament; it drives the church to be missional. Finally, baptism is inseparable from the Emmanuel motif: "I am with you always." The church enjoys the presence of Christ not without her mission to all nations. Baptism is a mark of a growing church for it reflects the continuity of Christ's authority, teaching, and presence on earth.

6.2. The Holy Supper

Reformed theology of the Lord's Supper is consistent with its baptismal theology. Both follow the Chalcedonian distinction between the two natures of Christ. The HC insists that "just as the water of baptism is not changed into Christ's blood . . . , so too the holy bread of the Lord's Supper does not become the actual body of Christ."[26] It is important to be able to distinguish between the visible signs and the invisible things signified in the Reformed tradition. Without this sound distinction, there is a real danger of confusing the two. When confusion happens, people are led into idolatry. Yet, on the other hand, the Reformed tradition also emphasizes the inseparability of bread/wine and body/blood of Christ. Referring to 1 Cor 10:16–17, the HC states, "we, through the Holy Spirit's work, share in his true body and blood as surely as our mouths receive these holy signs in his remembrance."[27] There is a real sharing/participation (κοινωνία) in the Lord's Supper. The HC accommodates Zwinglian tradition when it explains the meaning of eating the crucified body of Christ and drinking his blood:

26. HC 78.
27. HC 79.

"It means to accept with a believing heart the entire suffering and death of Christ"; yet, the Calvinian emphasis on the real union with Christ by the Holy Spirit is clearly identifiable: "But it means more. Through the Holy Spirit, who lives both in Christ and in us, we are united more and more to Christ's blessed body."[28] In his *Institutes*, Calvin wrote:

> For there are some who define the eating of Christ's flesh and the drinking of his blood as, in one word, nothing but to believe in Christ. But it seems to me that Christ meant to teach something more definite, and more elevated . . . It is that we are quickened by the true partaking of him; and he has therefore designated this partaking by the words "eating" and "drinking," in order that no one should think that the life that we receive from him is received by mere knowledge.[29]

Calvin did not mention Zwingli by name, yet we know that he criticized the Zwinglian tradition for its inadequate understanding of the signs of the Supper.[30] Calvin's criticism on "mere knowledge" is also noteworthy. In his theology of the Supper, he liked to include the importance of feeling and sensory perception.[31] There are potentials in Reformed sacramental tradition for our postmodern context that stresses the importance of embodiment in worship. Christian worship is not just contemplating certain eternal truths by the power of reason; it is also an experience that includes feeling, seeing, tasting, hearing, smelling, and touching. The beauty in the sacraments is that this (physical) sensory perception is not separated from spiritual seeing, tasting, hearing, etc. Through the visible signs, believers are transported to the invisible realm: the spiritual cleansing of the blood

28. HC 76.

29. Calvin, *Institutes*, IV.17.5.

30. As early as in his *Short Treatise on the Supper of Our Lord*, Calvin already wrote that the Lord's Supper "is not a bare figure but is combined with the reality and substance. It is with good reason then that the bread is called the body, since it not only represents but also presents it to us. Calvin, *Short Treatise on the Supper*, 16. Interpreting John 6:50–51, Zwingli wrote, "in this chapter Christ means by 'bread' and 'eat' nothing else than 'the gospel' and 'believe,' because he who believes He was slain for us and who relies on Him has eternal life; and that He absolutely is not speaking of sacramental eating." Zwingli, *The Latin Works*, vol. 3, 205.

31. For Calvin, the purpose of the mystical blessing in the Lord's Supper is "to confirm for us the fact that the Lord's body was once for all so sacrificed for us that we may now feed upon it, and by feeding *feel* in ourselves the working of that unique sacrifice." Calvin, *Institutes*, IV.17.1; italics mine; see also Calvin's interpretation on Eph 3:17 in *Inst.* IV.17.5.

and Spirit of Christ in the Holy Baptism and the spiritual eating and drinking of the body and the blood of Christ in the Holy Supper. Our bodily
participation and our spiritual understanding are thus fully integrated. To
quote once again from the HC:

> as surely as I receive from the hand of the one who serves, and
> taste with my mouth the bread and cup of the Lord, . . . so surely he
> nourishes and refreshes my soul for eternal life with his crucified
> body and poured-out blood.[32]

Bierma has pointed out the influences of both Melanchthon and Thomas
Erastus, a court physician in Heidelberg, on the importance of assurance
in the treatment of the Lord's Supper.[33] The motif of assurance had been
emphasized again and again not only in the Reformed but also in the
Lutheran-Melanchthonian tradition. For Welker, the expressions *given for
you—poured out for many* not only convey a deep and intense assurance but
also a highly concrete communal experience.[34] The church is a community
created and nourished by Christ. She is a receiving, not a self-sustaining
community. The expression *for many* communicates the ecumenical universality of the Lord's Supper: its celebration "creates a basic communion of
the ecumenical church . . . in all times and regions of the world."[35]

It is deeply saddening that the theology of the Lord's Supper has become the cause for Christian disunity! The spirit of exclusion or exclusive
communion by certain Christian denominations does not reflect the original teaching of Christ. Of course, not everyone benefits from the power of
the body and the blood of Christ in the Lord's Supper but only the elect;
yet a Eucharistic church is called to proclaim the universality of the death
of Christ: his blood is poured out for many! The exclusion of believers
from other Christian denominations betrays the very message of the Lord's
Supper. From a Reformed perspective, Christ himself (not the church)

---

32. ". . . daß Er selbst meine Seele mit seinem gekreuzigten Leib und vergossenen
Blut so gewiß zum ewigen Leben speise und tränke, als ich aus der Hand des Dieners
empfange und leiblich genieße das Brot und den Kelch des Herrn . . ." HC 75.

33. Melanchthon insisted on the dual function of the sacraments, i.e. of reminding
and of giving assurance (*admonere et confirmare*), while Erastus in his earlier work wrote
striking parallels with the HC: "*er speise und träncke so gewiss mit der gemainschafft seines
gekreuzigten leibs und vergossnen Blüts zum ewigen leben als gewiss wir brot und wein
empfahlen.*" Erastus, *Gründtlicher bericht*, 49; cf. Melanchthon, *Loci theologici* [1521],
209; see Bierma, *The Theology of the Heidelberg Catechism*, 74 and 84–85.

34. Cf. Welker, *What Happens in Holy Communion?*, 138.

35. Welker, *What Happens in Holy Communion?*, 142.

hosts the Lord's Supper and he calls all people to believe in him (not *in* the church) and to receive the forgiveness of sins.[36] The exclusion of those who believe in Christ from participating in one table communion with Christ is a grave sin. The keys of the kingdom are not exclusions of other Christian communions but church discipline. Thus the HC teaches, "Those who, though called Christians, profess unchristian teachings or live unchristian lives, . . . such persons the church excludes from the Christian community by withholding the sacraments from them . . ."; yet it then continues, "Such persons, when promising and demonstrating genuine reform, are received again as members of Christ and of his church."[37] The keys of the kingdom are not the arrogance of the bishops and priests to excommunicate Christians from other denominations but loving examinations of members of Christ in the church.[38] The hope of such church discipline is the inclusion of all repentant believers in one table fellowship with Christ.

In the midst of racism and any kind of ethnic supremacy or ethnic inferiority, the spirituality of the Lord's Supper gives a meaningful narrative of the universal sufficiency of the death of Christ. As in the Holy Baptism, the abolition of the distinction between races is made manifest in the Lord's Supper (cf. Gal 3:28; 1 Cor 12:13). Not that such distinction no longer exists, but that it does not create racial consciousness. Holy Baptism is the initiation rite that makes possible complete reception of all kinds of people into God's people, while the Lord's Supper is the celebration and commemoration of that universal reception. The commemoration of the broken body of our Lord in the Lord's Supper cannot be separated from the celebration of the same body being united. In Israel's understanding, commemoration is not merely recollection of the historical event. Commenting on the Passover in Exod 12, Fretheim rightly says:

> When Israel reenacts the passover, it is not a fiction, as if noth-
> ing really happens in the ritual, or all that happens is a recollec-
> tion of the happenedness of an original event. The reenactment
> is as much salvific event as the original enactment. The memory

36. Calvin carefully distinguished between "believe in" and "believe" regarding the relationship of church and creed. Cf. Calvin, *Institutes*, IV.1.2.

37. HC 85.

38. In his commentary on Matthew, St. Jerome wrote, "in the sight of God it is not the verdict of the priests but the life of the accused that is examined . . . This does not mean that the priests make them leprous and unclean, but that they have knowledge of the leprous and the non-leprous, and they can discern who is clean and who is unclean." St. Jerome, *Commentary on Matthew 16:19*, 192–93.

language (12:4; cf. 13:3, 9; Deut. 16:3) is not a "soft" matter, recalling to mind some story of the past. It is an entering into the reality of that event in such a way as to be reconstituted as the people of God thereby.[39]

There is no better way to express it. Such a high view of commemoration is far from empty symbolism or ritualism. On the contrary, it reenacts the salvific distribution of the one body of Christ. The Lord's Supper heals broken communities.

It is hard to overemphasize the ecumenical dimension of the Lord's Supper. Thus, the Leuenberg Agreement (1973) includes the universal aspect of the Lord's Supper in thesis 18:[40]

> In the Lord's Supper the risen Jesus Christ imparts himself in his body and blood, given up *for all*, through his word of promise with bread and wine. He thus gives himself unreservedly *to all* who receive the bread and wine; faith receives the Lord's Supper for salvation, unfaith for judgement.[41]

Yet, this universal aspect is not without differentiation: only those who believe receive the Lord's Supper for their salvation. The soteriological criterion is faith, not membership of a certain Christian denomination. Leuenberg also emphasizes the inseparable union between "communion with Jesus Christ in his body and blood" and "the act of eating and drinking."[42] The mystery of Christ's presence in the Lord's Supper is both affirmed and maintained. The Leuenberg Agreement may serve as a "unity in reconciled diversity" by declaring church communion between the Protestant churches in Europe understood as a communion of churches of different confessional status.[43] Such agreement does not negate the uniqueness of each Christian tradition. Rather, it encourages different Christian denominations to reflect on the common belief shared by all. At the table fellowship with Christ, we who truly believe in him become one.[44]

39. Fretheim, *Exodus*, 139.

40. Leuenberg Agreement is an ecumenical document, whose goal was to establish church fellowship among the Lutheran, Reformed, and United Churches in Europe. The agreement became the founding document of the Community of Protestant Churches in Europe. The community is a fellowship/communion of churches that includes almost all of the Lutheran, Reformed, and Methodist Churches in Europe.

41. Leuenberg Agreement, thesis 18; italics mine.

42. Leuenberg, thesis 19.

43. Harding Meyer, "Einheit in versöhnter Verschiedenheit," 100.

44. The claim that the table should be open to all should not be understood that the

What is the meaning of "this is my body . . . this is my blood" (Mark 14:22, 24)? It means that in the Lord's Supper, the church witnesses that just as the bread that we eat becomes one with our body, so we become one with the body of Christ. Believers feed on Christ as the bread of life (cf. John 6:57). His body is true food and his blood true drink (John 6:55). When believers spiritually eat the body of Christ, they become one with Christ. Believers are in an organic relationship one to another. Each member of the body is reminded of one's own function. Organic relationship stands in contrast with indifference or the pursuit of individual goals. In the organic relationship believers see the great vision of the church as the family of God. The Lord's Supper brings believers to see the reality of the kingdom of God instead of one's own kingdom. The Lord's Supper is inseparable from the second petition of the Lord's Prayer "Your kingdom come." When we pray for the coming of the kingdom, we confess the existing tension between *already* and *not yet*. On the one hand we are already joyful about the coming of the kingdom; on the other we should wait fervently for the eschatological meal and pray for the Maranatha.[45] The already-aspect encourages us in the midst of this fallen world, giving us enough reasons to be thankful for the foretaste of the kingdom, while the not-yet-aspect keeps us from the state of euphoria, reminding us to labor more faithfully for the coming of the kingdom.

Another tension in the Lord's Supper is between holy grief and holy joy. The Lord's Supper is both a sacrifice and a feast. Looking back, the Lord's Supper is a commemoration of the death of Christ; looking forward,

---

Leuenberg Agreement encourages both believers and unbelievers to partake of the Lord's Supper. It is rather a realistic description that the minister of the sacrament is not always able to know who truly believe and who do not. In his commentary, Calvin wrote, "I do not admit, that those who bring with them a mere historical faith, without a lively feeling of repentance and faith, receive anything but the sign. For I cannot endure to maim Christ, and I shudder at the absurdity of affirming that he gives himself to be eaten by the wicked in a lifeless state, as it were. Nor does Augustine mean anything else when he says, that the wicked receive Christ merely in the sacrament, which he expresses more clearly elsewhere, when he says that the other Apostles ate *the bread* — *the Lord*; but Judas only the *bread of the Lord*." Calvin, *Comm.* 1 Cor 11:27. What Calvin taught is that there is no such thing as the eating by the impious (*manducatio impiorum*) as taught by the Gnesio Lutherans, for those who do not believe do not eat Christ but only the bread. Even unbeliever such as Judas could partake of the Supper yet he did not eat Christ but only the sign. Precisely in this context, the Leuenberg also teaches that though the bread and wine can be received by all, "faith receives the Lord's Supper for salvation, unfaith for judgement." Leuenberg Agreement, thesis 18.

45. Cf. Welker, *What Happens in Holy Communion?*, 121–22.

it is an anticipation of the eschatological banquet. Calvin beautifully presented this creative tension between feast and sacrifice when he described the Lord's Supper as a sacrifice of thanksgiving.[46] In the Lord's Supper, believers learn to live the presence *between the times*, i.e. between Christ's sacrifice in the past and his glorious banquet in the future. In Christ alone, those who mourn shall be comforted (cf. Matt 5:4); Christ alone shall give the oil of gladness and the garment of praise instead of a faint spirit (cf. Isa 61:3). As a means of grace, the Lord's Supper creates a moment and space for godly grief that produces continuous repentance that leads to salvation (cf. 2 Cor 7:10). It also gives hope and courage to live the present life with gratitude and sacrifice.

The Lord's Supper is also a confession that Christ himself is the host. Bavinck points out that, unlike in the Passover meal, Christ "does not . . . take the bread and wine from the hand of others . . . , he himself takes . . . it from the table in proof that he is the host."[47] The church reflects and witnesses Christ's hospitality, not her own hospitality, let alone claims to be the host of the Lord's Supper. The church does not invite; she is invited to the Holy Supper by Christ. As in the story of the wedding at Cana, Christ revealed himself and his glory to be the true bridegroom, the true host of the wedding, for only he can provide the spiritual wine, the true joy that never runs out. In the wedding of Cana, water is characteristic of the old order, for it was used for Jewish purificatory rites; in contrast, wine is characteristic of the new order in Jesus.[48] Similarly, in the story of Zacchaeus—though it is not directly related to the Lord's Supper—it was Jesus who invited Zacchaeus so that he could receive Jesus at his house. Christ is not invited; he invites. The church should serve as an open and embracing community of the invited. She does not invite; she merely proclaims Christ's invitation and hospitality.

As the Reformers used to teach, the sacraments are *verba visibilia*. Frame elaborates, "they are also words that can be touched, smelled, and tasted. All our senses are engaged, filled with biblical content."[49] For Frame, the sacraments bridge the categories of word-and person-revelation. Carefully, we can also say that the Lord's Supper is not only *verbum visibilis* but also *Christus visibilis*, yet visible not by the physical but by the spiritual

---

46. Cf. Calvin, *Institutes*, IV.18.16.

47. Bavinck, *Reformed Dogmatics*, vol. 4, 575.

48. Beasley-Murray, *John*, 36.

49. Frame, *A Theology of Lordship*, vol. 4, 271.

eye. The Lord's Supper reminds believers that Christian *koinonia* should be visibly seen (and touched and smelled and tasted). It is a confession against docetic Christology and ecclesiology. In modern docetic ecclesiology Christ is merely contemplated, not touched, smelled, and tasted. In other words, it only enlightens the head but does not touch the heart. In the Lord's Supper, however, believers shall taste and see the goodness of the LORD" (cf. Ps 34:8). On this verse, Calvin commented:

> the Psalmist indirectly reproves men for their dullness in not perceiving the goodness of God, which ought to be to them more than matter of simple knowledge . . . there is nothing on the part of God to prevent the godly, to whom he particularly speaks in this place, from arriving at the knowledge of his goodness by actual experience.[50]

Experience, especially sensory experience is an important aspect in the celebration of the Lord's Supper. We taste, touch, smell, hear, and see the beauty of Christ. Calvin indeed criticized superstitious sensing when it is falsely claimed to give power for the forgiveness of sins.[51] However, believers understood that in sacramental eating, they taste spiritually as they also hunger spiritually.[52] The Lord's Supper liberates us from seeing things without any reference to Christ. This is not to say that everything is a sacrament but that nothing can be perceived in a naturalistic manner, i.e. without any relation to its Creator. On the contrary, from the visible order we should be moved and elevated to the invisible. The Lord's Supper teaches us that beyond the visible realm there is an invisible spiritual realm; beyond the taste of the bread, we taste Christ and his goodness. As has been said before, Reformed theology of the Lord's Supper follows the Chalcedonian distinction between Christ's two natures. In his emptying, Christ kept his Godhead "concealed for a time, that it might not be seen, under the weakness of the flesh," wrote Calvin.[53] Coherently, the Lord's Supper is a kenotic event: the beauty of Christ is concealed under the frailty of the bread in the Lord's Supper. His divine beauty is spiritually accessible for those who believe yet remains hidden for those who do not believe.

---

50. Calvin, *Comm.* Ps 34:8.

51. Cf. Calvin, *Inst.* IV.19.18.

52. Cf. Calvin, *Inst.* IV.17.34.

53. Calvin, *Comm.* Phil 2:7.

7

The Attributes of the Church

THE FOUR ATTRIBUTES OF the church are sometimes said to be in need of reconsideration. Allison, for instance, is not convinced that the same strange voices resisted by the early church are faced by the contemporary church today.[1] This is something that we, of course, hardly disagree with. Yet, we believe that the inclusion of the four classical attributes is neither less Reformed nor less evangelical,[2] for the Reformed *notae ecclesiae* had their root in the traditional four attributes of the church. Moreover, contemporary ecclesiological errors are nothing but the implications of the ancient Christological heresies.

7.1. Unity

The oneness or unity of the church is a reality given by God. Schism, on the contrary, is human made and constructed. When Paul spoke of "the church of God," he could apply the designation not only to the local congregation but also to the whole universal church (cf. 1 Cor 10:32; 11:22; 12:28). In 1 Cor 10:32, offense to Jews or to Greeks are considered an offense to the whole church. In 1 Cor 11:22, humiliating those who have nothing is despising the church of God. In 1 Cor 12:28, God's appointment of apostles,

---

1. Cf. Allison, *Sojourners and Strangers*, 104.

2. Against Ramsey, who, for instance, advises that our ecclesiological view had better be evangelical than archaeological. See Ramsey, *The Gospel and the Catholic Church*, 69.

prophets, teachers, and other spiritual gifts is not meant to be understood only in the local Corinthian congregation but in the church as a whole.

Though fellowship with the apostles in the New Testament provided a certain structural unity, the oneness of the church is more of a unity in one Spirit, in one body of Christ:

> There is one body and one Spirit—just as you were called to the one hope that belongs to your call—one Lord, one faith, one baptism, one God and Father of all, who is over all and through all and in all. (Eph 4:4-6)

A structural unity cannot guarantee the oneness of the church for this unity is a spiritual rather than an institutional unity. Paul urged the Ephesians to maintain the unity of the Spirit by walking with all humility, gentleness, patience, and love (cf. 4:2-3), i.e. the spiritual unity in all Christian virtues. There is always a temptation for the church to replace this spiritual unity by a mere structural unity. The author himself urged Ephesians to be one as a "prisoner for the Lord" (4:1). Far from being excluded from the unity, Paul could not view the oneness of the church without the perspective of Christian suffering.

The unity of the church is not characterized as one successful institutional organization but one fellowship in suffering for Christ's sake. A meaningful structural unity cannot exist without a fellowship in suffering. Paul was outside this communion when he persecuted the church of God (cf. 1 Cor 15:9). He called himself "a persecutor of the church" (Phil 3:6). The church of God (one and singular!), on the contrary, is a communion of suffering and persecution. Merely maintaining a hierarchical unity without suffering for Christ's sake is alien to Pauline ecclesiology. On the contrary, the church structural unity can be meaningful if the church understands herself as a fellowship in suffering and persecution for Christ. When we speak of persecution, we do not mean a pathological idealization of being persecuted in a continent with Christian majority. Rather, in a world that craves for institutional greatness and establishment, it is impossible for the church not to suffer for Christ's sake. The difference between the early church and the modern church is that the first was concerned to be faithful while ours is more preoccupied with numbers, influence, and power.[3] Today we would consider the church in Smyrna and Philadelphia to be

---

3. Cf. Osborne, *Revelation*, 129.

insignificant and full of tragedies, whereas in truth Christ himself praised them.

"Through many tribulations" the early church "must enter the kingdom of God" (Acts 14:22). She reflected the life of Christ who should suffer many things before entering into glory (cf. Luke 24:26). Paul longed to know Christ and the fellowship of his sufferings (cf. Phil 3:10). In the fellowship of Christ's suffering, the church is one. Division in the body of Christ is reversed when all members learn to suffer together (cf. 1 Cor 12:25–26). Suffering unites, (self-)glorifying divides. In the foretelling of his death, Jesus said that he must suffer many things and be rejected "by the elders and chief priests and scribes" (Luke 9:22). What caused them to reject and to kill Jesus? According to Luke, there are several reasons: Jesus cleansed the temple (cf. 19:45–48); he was teaching and preaching the gospel with authority (20:1–8); he told the parable of the wicked tenants against them (20:9–19); Jesus called his arrest their hour and the power of darkness (22:43); Jesus was acknowledged to be the Son of God (22:66–71); they accused Jesus for stirring up the people (23:4–5) and for misleading the people (23:14). In short, Jesus suffered because he continually criticized the religious establishment of the time and made people aware of its corruption. Had he made friends with these religious elites, Jesus would not have been killed.

If the church wants to maintain her unity, she must share Christ's sufferings by faithfully criticizing the danger of religious establishment, her own "establishment" included.[4] The way of Christ is the way to the cross, not the way to triumphant establishment in this world. Believers are strangers and exiles on the earth (cf. Heb 11:13; 1 Pet 1:1). "We walk by faith, not by sight" (2 Cor 5:7). Proving religious establishment that can be seen by physical eye is alien to Christian faith.[5] It is a path on which Christ never walked. Commenting on believers as strangers Calvin reminded of the meditation on the future life:

---

4. We use the term "establishment" here not in the context of a sound biblical establishment of the church throughout the history but in the context of the danger of conforming to the established political power instead of courageously suffering for the sake of Christ.

5. In this context Calvin rightly warned, "to embrace the unity of the church in this way, we need not . . . see the church with the eyes or touch it with the hands. Rather, the fact that it belongs to the realm of faith should warn us to regard it no less since it passes our understanding than if it were clearly visible." Calvin, *Inst.* IV.1.3.

But if they in spirit amid dark clouds, took a flight into the celestial country, what ought we to do at this day? For Christ stretches forth his hand to us, as it were openly, from heaven, to raise us up to himself. If the land of Canaan did not engross their attention, how much more weaned from things below ought we to be, who have no promised habitation in this world?[6]

The more a church seeks to establish her habitation in this world, the more she will be divided. The more she raises her mind up above the heavens, the more she understands her God-given unity.

The church is one because she is gathered by one Lord to the one and common faith, hope, and love (cf. Eph 4:5).[7] The unity of the church is based on Christ who is one and received through faith alone which is also one. From a Protestant perspective, perceiving the unity of the church through faith means that faith alone is the instrument of justification,[8] it is also the lone instrument of the unity of the church. Yet, as it is not alone in the justified person but ever accompanied with other virtues, so with regard to the unity of the church, faith is also accompanied with hope and love.[9] The unity of the church is not something done by herself, but something received and rested on the oneness of Christ through faith. Christ, by his oneness or undividedness, did fully terminate the disunity of all (true) churches,[10] and did make a real and full communion with the Father on behalf of the church.[11] This communion we receive through faith alone. On the other side, the unity of the church should be cherished with hope and love. A hopeful church moves towards full communion while seeking Christ's shalom to local, national, and global bodies of Christ's church.[12] A

6. Calvin, *Comm.* Heb. 11:13.

7. Cf. Gerhard, *Loci theologici*, Locus XI, 35; see also Schmid, *Doctrinal Theology*, 590.

8. Cf. WCF XI.2.

9. In this context, unity is not only parallel to justification but also to sanctification.

10. This seems to be an oxymoron (there is no disunity of true churches; for the attribute of the church is not disunity but unity); however, one needs to look at the church in Corinth (cf. 1 Cor 1:10–13) or Ephesus (cf. Eph 2:14–19). To borrow Healy's language, Paul did not just picture an idealized ecclesiology but addressed realistically and practically the concrete sinfulness of the churches.

11. The language is borrowed from WCF XI.3 to show the inseparability between the reality of justification (and sanctification) and the unity of the church.

12. Against the danger of schism, Fergus MacDonald proposes a strategy featuring five perspectives: theological, evangelical, psychological, sociological, and soteriological. Borrowed from Romans, the five-fold strategy pursues to overturn sectarian tendencies.

loving church learns to distinguish the essentials from the non-essentials, for we are called to be united, not uniformed.[13]

7.2. Holiness

As has been said, one of the most important attributes of the church is holiness. Holiness, first, belongs to God. God then bestows it upon his church. Webster laments the fact that in modern ecumenical ecclesiology, the attribute of holiness has been relatively little discussed. To speak of the holiness of the church is primarily "to indicate that it is the assembly of the *elect.*"[14] The church is holy because of her electedness and because she keeps indicating God's perfection in his election. This chosen community is gathered, protected, and preserved by Christ through his Spirit and Word.[15] Webster echoes the teaching of the church's holiness as had been handed down in the Protestant tradition. The Lutheran Orthodox theologian Johann Gerhard wrote:

> The Church is said to be *holy*, from 1 Cor. 14:33; Rev. 11:2; because Christ its head is holy, Heb. 7:26, who makes the Church partaker of his holiness, John 17:19; because it is called by a holy calling and separated from the world, 2 Tim. 1:9; because the Word of God, committed to it, is holy, Rom. 3:2; because the Holy Ghost in this assembly sanctifies believers by applying to them, through faith, Christ's holiness, working inner renewal and holiness in their hearts, and awakening in them the desire of perfect holiness.[16]

In short, the church is holy first of all because of the objective holiness of Christ. The church is the place wherein Christ communicates his holiness to be desired.

The holiness of the church is based on Christ's priestly office. Christ consecrates himself for the sake of the church that the church may be sanctified in the Word (cf. John 17:17, 19; Eph 5:26–27). In the HC, Christ's priestly office is explained in relation to his bodily sacrifice and his intercession.[17] The church points to Christ's priestly office by presenting herself

---

13. The principle of unity in diversity instead of uniformity is clearly attested in 1 Cor 12:14–20.

14. Webster, "On Evangelical Ecclesiology," 18.

15. Cf. HC 54.

16. Gerhard, *Loci theologici*, Locus XI, 36; quoted in Schmid, *Doctrinal Theology*, 590.

17. Cf. HC 31.

to him "as a living sacrifice of thanks."[18] Thus the holiness of the church is primarily the faithful attestation of the perfect sacrifice of Christ and through this testimony, inviting the people of God to sacrifice themselves like Christ. Parallel to justification, there is no talk of the holiness of the church without the sacrifice of Christ, on which the holiness of the church depends. Parallel to sanctification, true holiness then calls for consequent sacrifice.

The church is holy because the Father gave Christ to the church (cf. Eph 1:22) and the Holy Spirit for the true knowledge of God (cf. Eph 1:17). Yet, Christ was given to the church as the Head of the church, to whom the church owes submission and obedience. Pointing to the Lamb of God, who takes away the sin of the world, the church is called to mediate, to faithfully intercede for the world and plead its cause with Christ. The calling to mediate and to intercede is the calling of a peacemaker (cf. Matt 5:9). Just like presenting herself as a sacrifice of thanks is the church's response to Christ's sacrifice, so is the church's intercession a reflection and fellowship of Christ as the Great Intercessor. A holy church is a prayerful church.

The holiness of the church should not be confused with ecclesiastical perfectionism. Citing Matthew 13:47–58, Calvin reminded us that the church is a mixture of good and bad human beings.[19] Her imperfection is not an excuse for leaving the true church. Moreover, a holy church will bear patiently and rebuke lovingly her sinful children in Christ's sanctification. The parameter of the true holiness of the church is her unity. If a church keeps splitting (in the name of holiness), she does not yet understand the true holiness. Christ is holy and he communed with sinners and transformed them. Christ's church is to reflect his holiness.[20]

One important characteristic of a holy church is her courage to rebuke sins. This is to be distinguished from a judgmental church. A judgmental church sees the speck in the other's eye yet does not notice the log in her own eye (cf. Matt 7:1–3). A judgmental church does not exercise healthy self-criticism; she does not rebuke herself.[21] A courageous church, on the

18. HC 32.

19. Cf. Calvin, *Inst.* IV.1.13.

20. In practice, there will be a tension between holiness and unity. Should members, for instance, leave a church over scandalous sin? The answer will lead us to the essential question of what constitutes a true church. In other words, the answer depends on whether a certain church is still a true church or no longer a church.

21. Calvin reminded us of the danger of ungratefulness to God for the ministers of the Word who had courage to rebuke sins: "Those who think the authority of the Word is

contrary, points to the holiness of Christ and therefore faithfully rebukes sins, her own included. One of the dangers for the church today is the pressure of being politically correct. A politically correct church has lost her courage to proclaim the pure and holy doctrine of Christ.

Another important characteristic of a holy church is her honesty. According to a survey conducted by Barna Group, around 85% of Millennials do not go to church because they see Christians as hypocritical.[22] Far from being called to be superior, the church is called to witness the holiness of Christ along with all her weakness and vulnerability. Yet, she does not excuse, let alone theologically justify her weakness but honestly struggles to be sanctified by the Holy Spirit. Just as Christian theology should be vulnerable to the critique of the Holy Scripture,[23] so an honest church should also be submissive to the authority of Scripture.

Along with holiness, we can add two more attributes, namely, knowledge and righteousness. While holiness is closely related to Christ's priestly office, knowledge and righteousness are closely related to Christ's prophetic and kingly office. Just like holiness is an attribute *given* to the church, so knowledge and righteousness are bestowed upon the church. In Christ alone is the true knowledge of God; Christ alone is righteous. Just as her holiness, the knowledge and righteousness of the church are always of derivative character. Through her union with Christ, the church receives her holiness, knowledge, and righteousness.

We cannot understand the holiness of the church without true knowledge and righteousness. Parallel to justification, the church is holy because she has come to know, or rather to be known by the One who called her is holy (cf. Gal 4:9; 1 Pet 1:15). Parallel to sanctification, only by dedicating herself to the one true God can the church be sanctified. This is why *didaskalia* is essential to the holiness of the church, for without true knowledge of God the church cannot differentiate between sound biblical teachings and human ideologies. Theological illiteracy leads to idolatry. Nothing is further from holiness than idolatry.

---

dragged down by the baseness of the men called to teach it disclose their own ungratefulness." Calvin, *Inst.* IV.1.5.

22. Cf. David Kinnaman, "What Millennials Want When They Visit Church," *Barna Group*, 4 March 2015. Retrieved 23 December 2020, https://www.barna.com/research/what-millennials-want-when-they-visit-church.

23. Cf. Paul C. Maxwell, "What Is Vulnerable Theology?," *Patheos*, 24 June 2015. Retrieved 23 December 2020, https://www.patheos.com/blogs/paulcmaxwell/2015/06/24/what-is-vulnerable-theology/.

Coherently, holiness cannot be worked out apart from righteousness. As a holy priesthood (cf. 1 Pet 2:5), the church is called to practice righteousness. This practice is learned and made visible in the Lord's Supper for it is a witness that "Christ has invited all people and . . . shows an unparalleled hospitality that offers a future for all."[24] Partiality is an enemy of holiness for it betrays the universal invitation of Christ to all kinds of people. Multi-ethnic churches should be encouraged especially in the metropolitan cities where diverse ethnicities are to be found. In this context the attribute of holiness is inseparably related to catholicity.

7.3. Catholicity

Like holiness, the catholicity of the church has its basis in a divine attribute. The LORD is God of the universe, not a particular deity for a particular region. The catholicity of the church is a witness to the universality of the LORD. For Calvin, the catholicity of the church cannot be separated from the unity of the church, because Christ cannot be divided (cf. 1 Cor 1:13).[25] The church is one, because believers are all united in Christ. Calvin offered theological realism when he continued that the unity of the catholic church may be a small hidden remnant.[26] Thus, a triumphant visible body is not expected. The analysis of the catholicity that begins with the search for or a call for a united and universal visible body will end in a negative result; seeking the gift immediately in the recipient rather than in the giver will place an unbearable burden on the church.

This is not to say that we should not discuss the relationship between churches. Even if we seek the gift in God, we still have to discuss who are the true recipients of that gift. This leads us to the discussion on the true and false churches, or in other words, on when a church might cease to be a church. We refer precisely to these four attributes of the (true) church. A church belongs to the one holy catholic and apostolic church when she believes and reflects the marks of the church's unity, holiness, catholicity,

---

24. Van der Kooi and Van den Brink, *Christian Dogmatics*, 629.

25. Cf. Calvin, *Inst.* IV.1.2.

26. Similarly, the Belgic Confession teaches, "And this holy Church is preserved or supported by God against the rage of the whole world; though she sometimes (for a while) appears very small, and in the eyes of men, to be reduced to nothing; as during the perilous reign of Ahab, when nevertheless 'the Lord reserved unto Him seven thousand men, who had not bowed their knees to Ba'al.'" Belgic Confession, Art. 27.

and apostolicity. We are in communion with churches that, despite their diversity, confess the oneness of the church, despite their imperfection, refer to the holiness of the Triune God, despite their particular spatiality and temporality, claim for her catholicity, and despite their fallibility and sinfulness, show true signs of apostolicity.

If we should not begin with the search for a universal visible body, what should we start with? Echoing Calvin and the Belgic Confession, the WCF reminds us that the catholic or universal church is invisible while the visible church is also catholic or universal.[27] We should understand the church's invisibility here not in the sense of a *civitas Platonica* that considers any kind of embodiment as evil, but in the sense of spiritual hiddenness. Trying to establish the catholicity of the church in a physical manner betrays the spiritual (hidden and invisible) nature of the kingdom of God. The one church is called catholic because it is "spread abroad through all the parts and quarters of the world, and reaches unto all times, and is not limited within the compass either of time or place."[28]

The church's catholicity should not be understood in a limited localization but rather in its inseparable relation to the universal spreading of the gospel throughout the world. The catholicity of the church is not a static but a dynamic concept. Because the gospel of Christ is universal, therefore, the church should also be catholic in her witness and mission. She does not proclaim a particular "truth" for a particular region but the universal truth context-sensitively for every season and place. In this context, catholicity strongly relates to the vision of the kingdom of God. This vision views the church not as an ethnic community "confined to one nation as before under the law" but as a universal community composed of all kinds of nations and peoples.[29]

The church is not limited within certain time alone. We should neither lose perseverance during what the Belgic Confession called "the perilous reign of Ahab" nor boast that the works of God are most clearly manifested in our own time alone. The catholicity of the church teaches us to be humble in acknowledging the large spectrum of the kingdom of God on the one side and to be confident in God's faithful preservation of the church on the

27. Cf. WCF XXV.1–2. Rohls believes that there has been a shift of accent from the older to the newer Reformed confessions: while the former spoke of a chosen communion; cf. HC 54, the latter defined the church as "a communion of elect *individuals*." Rohls, *Reformed Confessions*, 167.

28. Second Helvetic Confession, XVII.2.

29. WCF XXV.2.

other. The Belgic Confession relates the temporal universality of the church to Christ's eternal kingship: "This Church hath been from the beginning of the world, and will be to the end thereof; which is evident from this, that Christ is an eternal king, which, without subjects He cannot be."[30] The belief in Christ's eternal kingship relativizes the belief of a certain era considered to be more glorious than the other and also encourages and comforts the church during times of difficulties and struggle.

According to the WRF Statement of Faith, central in the life of the church are "the worship of God, fellowship, the Holy Scriptures, the sacraments and mission."[31] The church's catholicity should be reflected in the universal understanding and practice of these five things. We can raise a few questions such as: What are the universal elements in a biblical worship? How can we articulate a more universal understanding of the sacraments and mission that in turn will deepen fellowship and cooperation between Christian bodies? With regard to worship, WRF answers that the worship of God "should include the singing of praise to God, the reading and preaching of Scripture and prayer."[32] Universal singing of praise can be done through compiling worship songs throughout the ages (temporal universality) and from all nations (spatial universality). Expository preaching in *lectio continua* has been a characteristic for Reformed churches since Zwingli; yet after some time (for instance, after a few years), it can be continued with the lectionary method with the benefit of the ecumenicity in expounding the same biblical passages at the same time for all churches. Thus, there is a time to preach with the expository method, and a time to preach with the lectionary.

With regard to prayer, it will be good if we can collect various prayers from different ages and places. Learning deferentially from theologies of the past has always been a habit of mind in the Reformed tradition.[33] Praying fervently with prayers from the past can enrich the church's understanding of her temporal universality. The church is catholic in her fervent prayers to Christ. Less praying churches do not have a healthy sense of ecumenicity for they are busy with their own agendas. It is interesting to note that the St. Petersburg revival cannot be separated from the theological framework

30. Belgic Confession, Art. 27.

31. WRF Statement of Faith, VIII.1.

32. WRF Statement of Faith, VIII.3.

33. Cf. Gerrish, "Tradition in the Modern World," in Willis and Welker, eds., *Toward the Future*, 13–14.

of Lord Radstock, the agent of the Spirit's movement during that revival. Radstock's framework grew out of the Pietistic-Puritan tradition in Britain in the nineteenth century that was characterized by a sense of evangelical ecumenicity.[34] This is not to say that doctrines are no longer important. Rather, during revival, strong spiritual passion has overcome confessional polemics and theological disputes that characterized Protestant Orthodoxy during the period of the Schmalkaldic War.

7.4. Apostolicity

The catholic church is finally apostolic in the sense that she can be based upon the apostolic teaching of Christ and his gospel. Mere historicity does not guarantee the apostolicity of the church. Rather, the church's apostolicity is primarily her faithfulness to the apostolic teaching. The early church believers "devoted themselves to the apostle's teaching and the fellowship" (Acts 2:42). The church as the household of God is "built on the foundation of the apostles and prophets," which is Christ Jesus himself (Eph 2:20). For Calvin, "foundation" here means the pure doctrine of Christ:

> But Christ is actually the foundation on which the church is built by the preaching of doctrine; and, on this account, the prophets and apostles are called builders. (1 Corinthians 3:10). Nothing else, Paul tells us, was ever intended by the prophets and apostles, than to found a church on Christ.[35]

The church is apostolic not because she is built on the apostleship but on the apostles' sole foundation, who is Christ.

It is interesting to note that some Reformed systematic theologies have no (or very little) discussion on the apostolicity of the church.[36] However, we believe that this fourth attribute is not less Reformed. Certainly, succession should not be understood in a physical sense for the reality of God's kingdom is a spiritual one. Coherent with this spiritual nature, the 'apostolic succession' can only be conceived as faithfully in line with the

34. Cf. Puzynin, "Lord Radstock," 100–117.

35. Calvin, *Comm.* Eph 2:20.

36. Thus, Hodge writes, "There is no command given in the New Testament to keep up the succession of the Apostles." Hodge, *Systematic Theology*, vol. 1, 140; Berkhof discusses the unity, the holiness, and the catholicity of the Church, but not the apostolicity. Cf. Berkhof, *Systematic Theology*, 572–76; Frame explains the apostolicity of the Church in less than one hundred words. Frame, *Salvation Belongs to the Lord*, 240–41.

apostolic teaching of Christ. The continuity with the early church is established when a church proclaims the same Christ and doctrine as had been
preached by the apostles. In the same sense, Bannerman writes:

> It is not the want of a spotless ecclesiastical genealogy, or of sac-
> raments derived by regular succession from primitive times, that
> will unchurch a Christian society, but the want of that apostolic
> doctrine which alone marks out a church of Christ.[37]

The church is not the highest authority to decide the right doctrine. Rather,
the right order is from the truth of Christ to the church, not vice versa.[38]

Similarly, the ecumenical theologian Edmund Schlink speaks of the
danger of self-preservation of the church.[39] A church can abuse her canon,
dogma, and order as a means of self-preservation. Self-preservation is a
human effort that does not reflect the belief in divine preservation. Such a
church either pompously claims her true apostolicity or anxiously preserves
her continuity with the past by her own power. In reality, Christ himself
preserves the continuity of his church. Rather than insisting on exclusivity,
churches can learn beautiful emphases from various theological traditions.
Advocating an ecumenical ecclesiology, Tjørhom argues for "various signs
of apostolic continuity" which are at hand in all churches such as justifying
grace, a vibrant worship life, accountable stewardship and mission, the role
of holiness in Christian life, the interconnection between faith and sacramental acts, appreciation of the work of the Holy Spirit, continuity with the
ancient church, and a modernized catholicity.[40]

From the evangelical Reformed perspective, the emphasis would fall
on the pure and faithful preaching and keeping of the apostolic gospel.[41]
According to the Second Helvetic Confession, the apostolicity of the church
should be differentiated from mere human traditions, which claim to be
apostolic. The signs of apostolicity are rather to be found in the apostolic

---

37. Bannerman, *The Church of Christ*, vol. 1, 60.

38. "It is the true faith that makes and marks the true Church, and not the true
Church that makes the true faith." Bannerman, *The Church of Christ*, 66.

39. "Nicht die Kirche erhält Gottes Wort, sondern Gott erhält durch sein Wort die
Kirche . . . Hat sie in diesem Glauben den Kanon gesammelt, Dogma und Ordnung
fixiert, so schließt das nicht aus, daß die Erhaltung durch Christus verkehrt wird in eine
Erhaltung der Kirche durch sich selbst und daß die Kirche Kanon, Dogma und Ordnung
als Mittel der Selbsterhaltung mißbraucht." Schlink, *Schriften zu Ökumene*, vol. 1, 103;
see also Schlink, *Schriften zu Ökumene*, vol. 2, 678.

40. Ola Tjørhom, "Better Together," 291–92.

41. Cf. Geneva Confession (1536), Art. 18.

teaching as had been taught in all churches (cf. 1 Cor 4:17), in the readable and understandable apostolic writing (cf. 2 Cor 1:13), and in the acts of the apostolic men in the same spirit and their same steps (cf. 2 Cor 12:18).[42] All of these signs are objectively verifiable. For Bullinger, the chief foundation of the apostolic doctrine is the doctrine of justification through faith, not through works.[43] The apostolic faith teaches the doctrine of Trinity: three persons distinguished from one another but with one and the same essence.[44] Christians believe the apostolic church by believing *in* the Holy Spirit as taught in the Constantinopolitan Creed.[45]

In this ecumenical width, Reformed theology is ready to learn various signs of apostolic continuity from other theological traditions. Not less important is to understand the church's apostolicity from a Christological perspective. The church is apostolic when she bears the marks of the apostles who were sent off by Christ. The word *apostolic* is from Greek ἀπόστολος with the verb ἀποστέλλω (send away or off). Christ himself was sent off by the Father on a divine mission (cf. Mark 9:37; John 3:17; Acts 3:20). Whoever receives Christ as the one who was sent by the Father receives the Father (cf. John 13:20). Christ's apostles were to be like Christ who received a little child in his arms (cf. Mark 9:36). A church is apostolic when she, like Christ, receives insignificant people. Paul the apostle was sent to preach the gospel with the power of the cross of Christ (cf. 1 Cor 1:17). The apostolic church is sent to preach the gospel, not with words of worldly wisdom but with the power of the cross. The apostolic church depends on the power of the One who has sent her into the world.

---

42. Cf. Second Helvetic Confession, II.

43. Bullinger, *Decade III. Serm. 9*, 325.

44. Bullinger, *Decade IV. Serm. 3*, 157.

45. Bullinger, *Decade I. & II. Serm. 9*, 158.

8

The Kingdom of God and Public Life

IN THIS FINAL CHAPTER we will discuss the relation between the church, the kingdom of God, and the public life. We start with some biblical theology on the kingdom of God. In historical theology, we will draw from Augustine, who developed a theology of the kingdom in his *City of God*. We will then proceed to a contemporary reading on Augustine's *City of God* by Healy. Since the kingdom of God cannot be perceived apart from the church, we will discuss the relation between the church and the kingdom. Here, Welker develops the threefold form (*Gestalt*) of the kingdom, which reflects Christ's threefold office. The discussion on the relation between the church and the kingdom will not be complete without discussing the Kuyperian and the 'two-kingdoms' approach. On what systematic theological basis can we assess both views? Is there any implication of this theological basis? We will then engage with Caputo as a representative of postmodern theologian who applies Derridean philosophy in his hermeneutics of the kingdom. Finally, a careful distinction between the spiritual and the political kingdom, between the church and the state is necessary in order to maintain a sound public theology from the Reformed perspective. This distinction is persuasively presented in Stackhouse's public theology.

The second part of the chapter discusses the role of the church in the public life. Here, we will seek a middle way between the two poles of theocracy and total separation. The first possible intermediary form is the Kuyperian and Dooyeweerdian idea. The second would be that of Hauerwas, who views the church as a counterculture. Can this countercultural approached be accommodated in the broader Reformed perspective? We will consult Stott and Radical Orthodoxy regarding this matter. Finally, we will consult Healy for his notions on the intraecclesial spiritual war as a corrective to the wrong countercultural approach. Does a church with continuous intraecclesial spiritual war cease to be a church? If not, what arguments can be offered?

8.1. The Kingdom of God

The Kingdom of God is presented as central to Jesus's teaching and can be found in the Four Gospels, Acts, and Pauline epistles. The secret of the kingdom of God had been given to the twelve, not to those outside (cf. Mark 4:11; Matt 13:11; Luke 8:10). The nearness of the kingdom demands repentance (cf. Matt 3:2). On the one side, the kingdom demands human responsibility, on the other it is graciously given by God to the poor in spirit and to those who are persecuted for righteousness sake (cf. Matt 5:3, 10). In the kingdom, the Torah is not abolished but done, taught, accomplished, and fulfilled (cf. Matt 5:17–19). For Matthew, entering the kingdom means doing better righteousness that exceeds that of the scribes and Pharisees. Through casting out demons, Jesus announced that the kingdom of God had already come (cf. Matt 12:28); yet, the disciples still ought to pray for the coming of the kingdom (cf. Matt 6:10). While Matthew related entering the kingdom to better righteousness, John related it to spiritual regeneration (cf. John 3:3, 5).

The church and the kingdom of God are inseparably related yet are not identical and must be clearly distinguished. While the church can have a territorial presence, the kingdom of God "is not coming in ways that can be observed," cannot be localized, but "is in the midst of you" (Luke 17:20).[1] Localizing the kingdom of God betrays its transcendental and eschatological nature. The church grows into and moves toward the kingdom of God. At the same time, the kingdom of God is truly in the midst of the church. The church should become like the children, to whom belongs the kingdom of God (cf. Luke 18:16), that is, to come to Jesus with nothing.[2] It is perhaps not a coincidence when later Luke wrote about the difficulty of those who had wealth to enter the kingdom of God (18:24). For a wealthy church it is difficult to enter the kingdom because she can have a lot of things to

1. The kingdom of God is localized in Christ's heavenly rule and will be localized in the new creation. It is not yet localized now in our experience.

2. Cf. Craddock, *Luke*, 212.

depend on! With such wealth, a church can fall into the temptation to make the kingdom of God appear visibly and immediately.

However, to the crowd who anticipated the immediate appearance of the kingdom of God, Jesus told the Parable of the Ten Minas (Luke 19:11–27). The kingdom of God is not about the immediate triumphant appearance of the kingdom but about the church's faithfulness. The church is like the LORD's servants, whom he gave ten minas and were asked to engage in business until he comes. Rather than impatiently trying to establish God's kingdom on earth, the church is promised to receive the power of the Holy Spirit upon her and to be Christ's witnesses in all the earth (cf. Acts 1:6, 8). The church is the witness of Christ, who went before her in proclaiming the good news of the kingdom where God rules over all aspects of life. In Acts, the narratives of the kingdom include baptism of male and female believers (cf. 8:12), going through many tribulations (cf. 14:22), encountering Jesus in Scripture (cf. 28:23), and teaching about him with all boldness (cf. 28:31). The church is closely related to the kingdom of God in that Christ, her head, is the person through whom God exercises his rule on earth.

In Pauline epistles, the kingdom of God is described in an antithetic manner. Thus, it does not consist in the talk of arrogant people but in the power of Christ (cf. 1 Cor 4:19–20). Those who will inherit the kingdom of God do not do the works of the flesh but walk and live by the Spirit, who produces his fruit (cf. Gal 5:16, 21–23, 25). Similar to Matthew though with a different theological profile, Paul associated the kingdom with righteousness, peace, and joy in the Holy Spirit rather than with a matter of eating and drinking (cf. Rom 14:17).

Historical-theologically, a detailed theology of the kingdom was arguably first developed by Augustine. Against the Donatists, Augustine carefully distinguished the church from the *civitas Dei*: the church on earth is not yet perfected. She is a *corpus permixtum* of true and false Christians.[3] In other words, she struggles with fears, sorrows, labors, and temptations.[4] Rejecting Eusebius's interpretation of church history, which he calls epic ecclesiology, Healy sees Augustine's concrete and dynamic ecclesiology as an anti-epic move.[5] Far from being static and settled, Augustine's ecclesiol-

---

3. Augustine, *City of God*, 1.35; 20.19.

4. Augustine, *City of God*, 18.49.

5. Borrowing from Hans Urs von Balthasar, Healy differentiates between the epic and the dramatic theology. Epic theology takes an external perspective upon the completed play while dramatic theology takes the perspective of a participant in the movement of the play and lives within it. Cf. Healy, *Church, World and the Christian Life*, 53–55.

ogy realistically includes the church's struggles, upheavals, and uncertainties during her pilgrimage on earth. The City of God is like Abel, who as a sojourner, built no city.

> For the city of the saints is above, although here below it begets citizens, in whom it sojourns till the time of its reign arrives, when it shall gather together all in the day of the resurrection; and then shall the promised kingdom be given to them, in which they shall reign with their Prince, the King of the ages, time without end.[6]

Though the church is not identical with the City of God, she is its representative. The kingdom of Christ will be fully revealed only at the eschaton.

In this present world, the church, following Abel, all the faithful prophets, Christ, and his apostles, has gone forward between "the persecutions of the world and the consolation of God."[7] The church on pilgrimage is a dialectical existence between persecution and consolation. Like Christ's apostles, she is "afflicted in every way, but not crushed; perplexed, but not driven to despair; persecuted, but not forsaken; struck down, but not destroyed" (2 Cor 4:8–9). In her affliction and persecution, the church shares in God's consolation through Christ (cf. 2 Cor 1:4–5). The church on earth is a comforted church; the heavenly church is a perfectly joyful church. Consequently, Augustine developed the distinction between *uti* (to use) and *frui* (to enjoy). While the earthly city worships gods with the goal of satisfying its lust of rule, the City of God worships God with the end of loving God. "The good use the world that they may enjoy God: the wicked, on the contrary, that they may enjoy the world would fain use God."[8] Unlike those of the earthly city, the citizens of the City of God find their true enjoyment in God and his kingdom. As the family of God, the church on pilgrimage may use the earthly good things without being detained by them (cf. 1 Cor 7:31).[9] The church should not be detained by earthly things because she is bound by Christ her head.

If Christ, the head of the church is the same Christ, through whom God rules, then we have to speak not only of a church Christology but also a public or kingdom Christology, for when God rules on earth, he rules not without his Christ. Drawing from Calvin's threefold office of Christ, Welker develops the threefold form (*Gestalt*) of the kingdom of God: the

6. Augustine, *City of God*, 15.1.

7. Augustine, *City of God*, 18.51.

8. Augustine, *City of God*, 15.7.

9. Augustine, *City of God*, 1.29.

kingly, the prophetic, and the priestly form.[10] He reminds us of the dangers brought by overweighting just one office. Thus a strong emphasis on the kingly office can develop energetic diaconal ministry yet at the same time bring the humanistic self-secularization of the church; a strong emphasis on the prophetic can develop astute academic-analytical theologies yet lead to spiritual exhaustion; a strong emphasis on priestly office can develop strong spiritual profiles yet lead to ecclesiocentric self-isolation. Welker argues for the observation of the perichoretic connection of the threefold form of the kingdom of God.[11] A perichoretic connection will help the church to witness to the relation between Christ's righteousness, true knowledge of God, and rich spirituality of thankfulness. Commenting on Welker, Reichel writes that in their mutual constructive and critical complementarity, *martyria, leitourgia,* and *diakonia* make up the Christian witness that faithfully refers to Christ's threefold office.[12]

First, the church is to proclaim and to witness the coming of the kingdom in her hunger and thirst for righteousness. The church should hunger and thirst both that she "may be righteous" and that "justice may be done everywhere."[13] In Matthew's theological profiles, "better righteousness" is identical with the Golden Rule (cf. Matt 7:12) that attains concrete form in deeds of mercy (cf. Matt 23:23) and in the love of God and neighbor (cf. Matt 22:37–39).[14] In James, practicing righteousness means that the church should show no partiality as she believes in Christ, the Lord of glory (cf. Jas. 2:1). The church's vision of the true glory in Christ will save her from seeing the false glory of a rich person. Like the Gospel of Matthew, the Book of James relates righteousness (in James' context: showing no partiality) with fulfilling the royal law, that is, the love of neighbor (cf. Jas. 2:8–9). In the modern context of a church that develops a corporate model, showing partiality toward rich persons can become a temptation; however, the church is called to hunger and thirst for righteousness.

---

10. Cf. Welker, *God the Revealed,* 209–10.

11. "Perichoretic" comes from "perichoresis," a term borrowed from the Trinitarian discourse. Perichoresis describes the relationship, the interpenetration, or the mutual indwelling between the three persons of the Trinity. In the High Priestly Prayer, Jesus said that the Father is in him, and he in the Father (cf. John 17:21). Perichoretic relationship maintains both the distinction and the unity or inseparability of the three persons.

12. Reichel, "Der Christ als Christus," in *Gottes Geist,* 34.

13. Carson, "Matthew," 134.

14. Cf. Schnelle, *Theology of the New Testament,* 446.

Hunger and thirst for righteousness also means that the church should function as a "prophetical-critical mirror before those who govern."[15] The church is to rebuke any form of unjust government resulting in the privileging of certain groups of people. It should be noted that the goal of the prophetic function of the church is not only to bring about change and transformation from unjust to just government but also to reflect Christ's righteousness in this fallen world. The church is blessed not because she triumphantly makes significant changes in the kingdom of the world; she is blessed when she is persecuted for righteousness sake, for hers is the kingdom of heaven (cf. Matt 5:10). McClean rightly criticizes the Kuyperian approach for its underemphasis on the eschatological tension between the already and the not yet of the kingdom, thus failing to avoid over-realization and to adequately represent an eschatological realism.[16] A Christian view of the fallen world is like our treatment of human bodies according to McClean: we still care for the sick even we know that death and pain are unstoppable.

The church is called to care for the poor even though "the poor you always have with you" (John 12:8); she is called to heal the sick like Jesus who came to heal the sick and the wounded. For Caputo, this is the true meaning of power displayed by Jesus: the power of healing others, of forgiveness, of mercy, of generosity, in short, the "power of powerlessness."[17] Drawing from Derrida, Caputo considers deconstruction as "the hermeneutics of the kingdom of God." Announcing the kingdom of God is like the good Samaritan who had compassion and proved to be a neighbor to the man who fell among the robbers. Jesus was the Good Samaritan who used his power not to save himself but to save others.[18]

The hermeneutics of the kingdom will help the church not to misunderstand Christ's kingship. "Rulers of the Gentiles lord it over them, and their great ones exercise authority over them" (Matt 20:25), but the greatness of Christ's disciples lies in their servanthood. Commenting on this verse, Calvin compared Israel's kings who used a scepter, crown, and throne to the pastors who are allowed to govern the church as nothing more than ministers.[19] Clearly, Calvin distinguished between the spiritual government

15. Van der Kooi, *Christian Dogmatics*, 637.

16. Cf. McClean, "Neo-Calvinism versus Two-Kingdoms," 184–85.

17. Caputo, *What Would Jesus Deconstruct?*, 84.

18. Cf. Caputo, *What Would Jesus Deconstruct?*, 85.

19. Cf. Calvin, *Comm.* Matt 20:25.

of the church and the government of the worldly empires. In Christ's kingdom, the dispute over the primacy of the servants of God shall not exist.
In his *Institutes*, Calvin discussed the two kingdoms doctrine in relation to
the nature of conscience. Conscience is instructed by the spiritual kingdom
while education for the duties of humanity and citizenship by the political
kingdom.[20] If the church is governed as a political kingdom, she will make
meaningless laws that hinder conscience of the believers that should only
be ruled by Scripture. Rather than oppress it with multitude useless observances, church laws should encourage pious conscience to reach Christ.[21]

Confusing the church with a political kingdom is the result of the
church's failure to distinguish between the spiritual and the political kingdom. Vice versa, the calling of the state is not to be confused with the
church's calling. The state deals with crime, not with every sin.[22] To rebuke
the latter is the calling of the church, not the state. A state that imposes
regulations on every sin runs the risk of becoming a theocratic state. A
good public theology will give space for freedom which includes the possibility of sinning and disobeying God. To quote Stackhouse:

> A God who leaves no place for error, contrition, and free choosing
> of what is right and good is not a God who can touch the core
> of human existence, just as no social arrangement that destroys
> freedom in a totally regulated environment can sustain human
> loyalty.[23]

There will be no genuine loyalty and devotion without any room for the
possibility of disobeying the law of God. The calling of the state is to guarantee human freedom, including freedom of religion, humbly acknowledging it as a gift of God.

Later, Stackhouse reminds us that humans cannot rely on freedom
when it is none other than "naturalistic urges" that occur from the trans-
fer of God's authority to nature's authority.[24] Without the presumptions of

---

20. Calvin, *Inst.* III.19.15.

21. Calvin, *Inst.* IV.10.11.

22. Stackhouse writes, "A public theology marks the delicate relationship of freedom
and sin by making a rather sharp distinction between sin and crime. Not all things that
are sinful should be seen as crimes. Public authorities are not competent to evaluate a
wide range of sins, and governments must exercise great restraint at this point." Stackhouse, *Public Theology*, 30.

23. Stackhouse, *Public Theology*, 30.

24. Stackhouse, *God and Globalization*, vol. 2, 27–28.

spiritual and theological insights, professions and regencies will have no development that augments "human freedom" because of their lack of "a conscious moral rudder."[25] It is true that some theological schools can turn toward stricter ethical practices yet the enduring relevance of theology cannot be simply wiped out by secularization. The "ascendency of nature," as Stackhouse calls it, has changed the nature of human freedom as God's gift into something autonomous. When the institutions of society assert autonomy from God's rule, the church that has a particular calling in spreading awareness of the reality of the kingdom can inspire them with an awareness that they are under universal moral laws and dedicated to a more ultimate purpose.[26] Stackhouse believes that God's creational and providential common graces are able to actually improve the dynamics and patterns of globalization, which reveals the impacts of the kingdom's inauguration by Christ.

We conclude as follows: in the Scripture, the church is not simply identified with the kingdom of God; however, she plays a central role in the kingdom. The narratives of the kingdom are continuously at war with the worldly narratives. Augustine drew a sharp contrast between the City of God and the earthly city. Understanding the antithetical character of the kingdom means that the church participates in the movement of the battle. Yet, the narratives of the kingdom are not only about antithesis but also about balance. We can obtain the balance by equally emphasizing the threefold form of the kingdom such as developed by Welker. A perichoretic connection of the threefold form equally emphasize caring for the poor, astute theological reflections, and strong spiritual profiles. In addition to the antithesis and balance, the kingdom of God also presents a paradoxical tension between the already and the not yet as it is exemplified in the church's diaconal ministry. Though we do not share his general theology, we agree with Caputo when he deconstructs Jesus's power of powerlessness as the hermeneutics of the kingdom. Finally, a sound Reformed ecclesiology should provide a careful distinction between the spiritual and the political kingdom such as presented in Stackhouse's public theology.

25. Stackhouse, *God and Globalization*, vol. 2, 29.
26. Cf. Stackhouse, *God and Globalization*, vol. 4, 228.

8.2. Public Life

The relationship between the church and public life is usually discussed within the spectrum of the theocratic idea, the total separation of church and state, and intermediary forms in between these two. Current theocracies include the Roman Catholic Vatican City and the Eastern Orthodox Mount Athos. Iran is an example of Islamic theocracies, while Indonesia, the country with the largest Muslim-majority rejects the theocratic idea as its political ideology. As for the Reformed tradition, scholars differ in their opinions as to what extent Calvin's Geneva was a theocracy. Evaluating the extent compels us to understand Calvin's idea of religious tolerance in Geneva. Calvin's successor, Theodore Beza, went further than Calvin when he taught that although *lex iudicialis* was valid only for the Jews yet it is principally unlimited in time.[27] While the theocratic belief in the lasting normative function of God's judicial law can be found in the Reformed tradition, separation of church and state has its root in the Anabaptist tradition. The radical reformers Michael Sattler and Menno Simons were the most important proponents of this alternative. Separation of church and state became more common in the course of the European Enlightenment and secularization. The French philosopher Denis Diderot famously said, "The distance between the throne and the altar can never be too great. In all times and places experience has shown the danger of the altar being next to the throne.[28]"

One of the possible intermediary forms between theocracy and total separation is the Kuyperian idea that acknowledges the plurality of worldviews and allows each community to develop its own institutions for some spheres in Dutch society.[29] Sadly, under the strong influence of secularization, the organizational structures of the conservative Reformed became increasingly a withdrawing approach from the public life to affirm one's own tradition.[30] Here we see that establishing one's own institutions

---

27. Cf. Beza, *De haereticis*, 221–22; see also Strohm, "Calvin and Religious Tolerance," 190. Strohm observes that although the strict Pentateuch laws against heresy provided Calvin with a model for using capital punishment to fight heretics, Calvin principally viewed the Old Testament judicial law as being no longer applicable to Christians.

28. Denis Diderot, *Political Writings*, 83.

29. Pillarization is a segregation of a society into groups based on religion or political beliefs. As a label, later sociologists invented the metaphor of pillarization (*verzuiling*), which was never used by Kuyper himself.

30. Cf. Van der Kooi, *Christian Dogmatics*, 636.

cannot hold back the wave of secular ideologies in Europe. The spirit of withdrawal is never compatible with the Reformed tradition which believes that the world is the place where we fulfil our cultural mandate. Moreover, establishing one's own structures should coherently allow other religious groups, e.g. Muslim immigrants in Europe, to create their own religious structure of society, something that conservatives might not be prepared for. Founding Christian political parties, broadcasting organizations, newspapers, schools, hospitals, trade unions are one thing, preparing the other church members who cannot participate in those structures is another thing. Christians do not live in a monastic ghetto but in the world, whose salt and light we are. Establishing our own structure and institution can easily be transformed into a religious ghetto that fails to salt and illuminate the world by idolizing one's own comfort zone. Reformed churches should not only build Reformed institutions for education, health, service, etc. but also prepare their congregation to dissolve and give taste in the fallen world.

Kuyper's idea was later developed by Dooyeweerd. Dooyeweerd's contribution can help to distinguish differentiated sovereignty or responsibility (*gespreide verantwoordelijkheid*) among the various spheres.[31] He defined fifteen modal law-spheres or modal aspects understood not only as categories but primarily as ways of functioning.[32] Dooyeweerd's theory of aspects is relevant in the discussion on the relation between the church and public life, because we need to understand the special responsibility of the church among other spheres or agents in our polymorphic society. The failure to understand the church's specific calling can lead to either a sense of superiority above other spheres or inferiority below them. Even when theology is no longer the queen of the sciences, it should not allow itself to be marginalized and ignored in the public sphere.[33]

---

31. The concept of differentiated responsibility teaches that polymorphic society consists of a diversity of responsible spheres or agents (such as the church, the court, the museum, the corporation, the educational institution, etc.). Each of these agents has a special responsibility or calling, which is different from one another.

32. These are the arithmetic, spatial, kinematic, physical, biotic, psychic, analytical, formative, lingual, social, economic, aesthetic, juridical, ethical, and pistic aspect.

33. Volf insists that though theology in a post-Christian context can no longer retain traces of nostalgia for its position in the center, it should rejoice its inhabited social space, which is the margins, for from the margins, theology can still exercise its role in the light of the coming kingdom of God. Volf, "Theology, Meaning and Power," in *The Future of Theology*, 113.

One of Dooyeweerd's most important contributions is his principled antireductionism, which serves as a correction against idolatry.[34] It is the calling of the church to be able to detect idolatrous ideologies in society that are substantially reductions of multifaceted reality. Dooyeweerd's theory of modal aspects also helps to distinguish things in the various spheres.[35] In Dooyeweerd's modal aspects, the church is of course expected to offer a modal analysis from the perspective of her ethical and mainly her pistical aspect. Without the ethical and pistical aspect of the church, the world will fail to understand itself in its totality by its tendency to fall into reductionism. Science, for instance, will never be able to offer the pistical aspect of reality, for it is not its responsibility.

No less important, the church must always be aware of her limited responsibility or calling: she is not to offer perspectives of modal aspects that particularly belong to other spheres, let alone to understand herself in terms of wrong modal aspects, e.g. as an arithmetic (with regard to her number), or kinematic (with regard to her movement), or historical (with regard to her culture) reduction. Thus, maintaining the unique responsibility of the church primarily according to her number, for instance, is a reduced way of describing the church. Surely the church possesses a certain numerical aspect yet it is not the most crucial function of the church. The most crucial function or responsibility of the church is to offer the ethical and mainly the pistical aspect of reality. The church is unique in public life, for she can offer certain modal aspects that cannot be offered by other agents in society. Dooyeweerd's idea, which expands Kuyper's reflections, is surely a very important Reformed intermediary form between theocracy and total separation.

Though not coming from the Reformed tradition, the other intermediary form is that which views the church as a counterculture. One of the most important proponents of this form is Stanley Hauerwas. The church's role in the public life is to be an alternative community to the world. This

---

34. Cf. Koyzis, *Political Visions*, 235. Koyzis lists a few examples: Marxist socialism is a kind of economic reduction, nationalism a biological or a lingual reduction, etc. Thus, in Marxist socialism, reality is conceived merely as economic. Surely this is a reduction, for reality is multifaceted and functioning in various modal aspects.

35. Cf. Koyzis, *Political Visions*, 240. Koyzis gives the distinction between an honorary medal and a coin as an example. Thus, a medal and a coin should be distinctively qualified according to the modal analysis: to the functioning of the first, the jural aspect is especially crucial while to the latter's functioning, the economic aspect. To qualify an honorary medal primarily according to the economic aspect is to reduce drastically the function of the medal.

alternative is a political alternative as was demonstrated in Jesus's political death. Hauerwas famously proposes an oft-cited aphorism: "The church is a political institution calling people to be an alternative to the world. That's what the cross is about. The first social task of the church is not to make the world more just; it's to identify the world as the world."[36] Jesus was killed not because of God's will that we love one another but because he courageously challenged the worldly powers. Following Jesus, the church as an alternative community is to be a witness to Christ. It is rightly noted that this approach consciously leaves behind the quest for relevance that has plagued the church in her strategies to transform the world.[37] Does this quasi-apolitical attitude in fact support the status quo in society? Hauerwas would answer that with the broader context of the gospel, Christian love will not end up as a sentimental support for the societal status quo but its prophetic challenge.[38] There is an element of truth in Hauerwas's emphasis on the role of Christian community. Even the authority of the Scripture's story cannot be attested apart from its practical function in the church community.[39]

The church as a counterculture has its root in Christ's Sermon on the Mount.[40] It is a counterculture, for it represents the reversal motif of the kingdom of God. Not the materially rich but the poor in spirit are blessed; not those who laugh but those who mourn are blessed, etc. When the church fails to function as a counterculture, young people will look "for the right things . . . in the wrong places."[41] The church is the focus of God's transforming power, not in the sense that she should not function as salt and light in the world, but that she is to be a witness of that transformation. Expecting the world to be a better place runs the risk of ignoring the fallen reality of the present life. Even Christ himself did not change the misuse of God's house for a den of robbers after he cleansed the temple. The temple was finally destroyed as had been foretold by Christ. The chief priests and

---

36. Hauerwas, "Christianity: It's not a Religion, It's an Adventure" (1991), in *The Hauerwas Reader*, 533.

37. Van der Kooi, *Christian Dogmatics*, 638.

38. Cf. Hauerwas, "Love's Not All You Need" (1972), in Hauerwas, *Hauerwas Reader*, 673.

39. Cf. Hauerwas, *Community of Character*, 95; see also Kristanto, "The Bible," 164.

40. Stott writes, "To my mind no two words sum up its intention better, or indicate more clearly its challenge to the modern world, than the expression 'Christian counter-culture.'" Stott, *The Message of the Sermon on the Mount*, 14–15.

41. Stott, *Sermon on the Mount*, 16.

the scribes "were indignant" (Matt 21:15); they challenged and questioned his authority (cf. Matt 21:23). However, the blind and the lame who came to him were healed and the children cried out, "Hosanna to the Son of David!" (Matt 21:14–15). The church is a community of the blind, the lame, and the children: she is not called to transform 'the chief priests and the scribes', i.e., those who challenge Christ's authority, but to come to Christ to be healed and to praise him. The church is an alternative community, a countercul-ture, because she acknowledges her sickness and disability, her needs to be healed by Christ, and her praise and thanksgiving for his wonderful deeds.

The church as a countercultural narrative community is also strongly advocated in Radical Orthodoxy. Cultural pessimism partly influences its ecclesiocentrism: deep immersion in the church is presupposed when one wants to live faithfully in a radically secularized culture.[42] However, such commitment further presupposes a total opposition between the *civitas terrena* and the *civitas Dei*. As one of the most important leading voices of Radical Orthodoxy, Milbank, for instance, is ambiguous in his view on violence. On the one hand, he maintains that violence can be rooted out from the church practice of forgiveness; on the other, he concedes that for the benefit of a substantive *telos*, violence may be justified.[43] In the practice of forgiveness, violence is to be opposed yet opposition itself is a form of counterviolence, which is redemptive. Boersma rightly questions that if violence can be redemptive, then it will call into question "the character of the church as a counterculture."[44] Just as nonviolence can find its way into the *civitas terrena* (in line with the Reformed doctrine of common grace), so violence can be associated with the *civitas Dei* (whether in a redemptive or in an evil sense). In the latter sense, the church is not a counterculture against the world or the public domain but a counterculture against her own sinful tendency. Understanding the church as a counterculture against the world runs the risk of ignoring the fallibility of the church.[45]

42. Cf. Chaplin, "Suspended Communities or Covenanted Communities?," in Smith and Olthuis, eds., *Radical Orthodoxy*, 174.

43. Cf. Milbank, *The Word Made Strange*, 251; Milbank, *Being Reconciled*, 38; see also Boersma, *Violence, Hospitality, and the Cross*, chap. 10.

44. Boersma, "Being Reconciled," in Smith and Olthuis, eds., *Radical Orthodoxy*, 200.

45. There are differences between the church being a healthy counterculture and be-ing monastic and separating from the world. The first sees the church as realistically sinful yet forgiven in Christ while the latter sees the church as the perfect agent of truth; the first sees the world as loved by God and in need of its Savior, the latter sees the world beyond redemption.

In the same tenor, Healy maintains that in the concrete, the church and the world are mutually constitutive so that spiritual war is to be anticipated not only against the world but also within the church:

> The church is a body that must struggle to understand its role, in part because Christianity is an essentially contested concept, and in part because it must continually purge itself of anti-Christ elements and appropriate, modify or reject non-church elements as it seeks to witness faithfully to the gospel. Such intraecclesial conflict should not be avoided by enforcing unity, for it may frequently be fruitful.[46]

The fruitfulness of intraecclesial spiritual war is the result of none other than the church's healthy self-criticism. There is thus a danger of false unity, false harmony, or false fellowship, i.e., a togetherness that discourages the church to be practical-prophetic against her own sinfulness. The church is not immune from neo-Marxism, capitalism, monetization, self-secularization, self-radicalization, self-actualization/realization, machoism, triumphalism, tribalism, etc. The true prophets in the Old Testament faithfully rebuked the people of God for their failure in justice and social responsibilities, in protection of the weak, and in the cultic life/true worship of God. As the culmination, Christ as the true prophet rebuked false righteousness, mercilessness, hypocrisy, superficial or outward religiosity, nationalist exclusivism, inhospitableness, and many others.

We conclude as follows: the role of the church in the public life should be found in the middle way between theocracy and total separation. There are at least two alternatives: one that has its root in the Reformed tradition and the other in the Anabaptist. Despite having similarities with the Anabaptist tradition, the countercultural approach in Hauerwas and in Radical Orthodoxy can be accommodated in the broader Reformed ecclesiological perspective, for it has its root in the Sermon on the Mount. We have to be aware, however, that the church's countercultural approach is not only directed against the world, but also against the church's own sinfulness. Despite her weakness and her intraecclesial spiritual war, the church does not cease to be the true church, because she is in becoming in her eschatological hope in Christ.

The church is to follow Christ, who will "not cry aloud or lift up his voice, or make it heard in the street," in the public but "bring forth justice to the nations . . . till he has established justice in the earth" (Isa 42:1–2, 4;

---

46. Healy, *Church, World and the Christian Life*, 70.

cf. Matt 12:18–20). "Living as a minority without a voice is often part of the mission of the church," reminds McClean rightly.[47] Instead of grumbling about her waning relevance in the public domain, the church should secure her confidence in her faithful reference to Christ, in him who promised, "Behold, I am making all things new" and "behold, I am coming soon" (Rev 21:5; 22:7). The church is not a static being, whether it is the family of God, the bride of Christ, the body of Christ, or any other metaphor. Rather, she is in becoming, growing into deeper union with her bridegroom, her head, truthfully and humbly participating in the kingdom of God and of his Christ. The church must always be reformed according to Christ alone. *Solus Christus.*

47. McClean, "Neo-Calvinism," 186.

Bibliography

Allison, Gregg R. *Sojourners and Strangers: The Doctrine of the Church*. Wheaton, IL: Crossway, 2012.

Anderson, David W. "Shepherding Souls and the Life of Faith." *Currents in Theology and Mission* 46 (2019) 50–54.

Augustine of Hippo. *The City of God*. In *St. Augustin's City of God and Christian Doctrine*. Vol. 2. Edited by Philip Schaff. Buffalo: Christian Literature Company, 1887.

Bannerman, James. *The Church of Christ: A Treatise on the Nature, Powers, Ordinances, Discipline, and Government of the Christian Church*. Vol. 1. Edinburgh: T. & T. Clark, 1868.

Barth, Karl. *Church Dogmatics*. Vol. III/2, *The Doctrine of Creation*. Edinburgh: T. & T. Clark, 1960.

Bauckham, Richard J. *Jude, 2 Peter*. WBC 50. Waco: Word, 1983.

Bavinck, Herman. *Reformed Dogmatics*, vol. 4: *Holy Spirit, Church, and New Creation*. Grand Rapids: Baker Academic: 2008.

Beale, G. K. *The Book of Revelation*. Grand Rapids: Eerdmans, 1999.

Beasley-Murray, G. R. *John*. WBC 36. Dallas: Word, 2002.

Berkhof, Louis. *Systematic Theology*. Grand Rapids: Eerdmans, 1938.

Bernard, Saint. *Sermons on the Canticle of Canticles*. Translated by a priest of Mount Melleray. Vol. 1. Dublin: Browne & Nolan, 1920.

Beza, Theodore. *De haereticis a civili Magistratu puniendis libellus, aduersus Martini Bellii farraginem, et novorum Academicorum sectam*. 1554.

Bierma, Lyle D. *The Theology of the Heidelberg Catechism: A Reformation Synthesis*. Louisville: Westminster John Knox, 2013.

Bock, Darrell L. *Luke*. Vol. 1: *1:1–9:50*. Grand Rapids: Baker, 1994.

Boersma, Hans. *Violence, Hospitality, and the Cross: Reappropriating the Atonement Tradition*. Grand Rapids: Baker, 2004.

Boring, M. Eugene. *Revelation*. Interpretation. Louisville: John Knox, 1989.

Brown, David. "Church, World and the Christian Life: Practical-Prophetic Ecclesiology." *Journal of Theological Studies* 52 (2001) 982–83.

Bullinger, Heinrich. *The Decades of Henry Bullinger: The First and Second Decades*. Edited by T. Harding. Cambridge: Cambridge University Press, 1849.

———. *The Decades of Henry Bullinger: The Third Decade*. Edited by T. Harding. Cambridge: Cambridge University Press, 1850.

————. *The Decades of Henry Bullinger: The Fourth Decade.* Edited by T. Harding. Cambridge: Cambridge University Press, 1851.

Busch, Eberhard, et al. *Calvin-Studienausgabe.* Vol. 2: *Gestalt und Ordnung der Kirche.* Neukirchen-Vluyn: Neukirchener, 1997.

Calvin, John. *Calvin's Commentaries: Psalms.* Electronic ed. Albany: Ages Software, 1998.

————. *Commentary upon the Acts of the Apostles.* Albany, NY: Ages Software, 1998.

————. *Institutes of the Christian Religion: 1536 Edition.* Translated by Ford Lewis Battles. Grand Rapids: Eerdmans, 1995.

————. *Institutes of the Christian Religion: 1541 French Edition.* Translated by Elsie Anne McKee. Grand Rapids: Eerdmans, 2009.

————. *Institutes of the Christian Religion.* 2 vols. Edited by J. T. McNeill. Translated by Ford Lewis Battles. Louisville: Westminster John Knox, 2011.

————. *John Calvin: Writings on Pastoral Piety.* Edited by Elsie Anne McKee. Classics of Western Spirituality. New York: Paulist, 2001.

Caputo, John D. *What Would Jesus Deconstruct? The Good News of Postmodernity for the Church.* Grand Rapids: Baker Academic, 2007.

Carson, D. A. *The Gospel according to John.* Grand Rapids: Eerdmans, 1991.

————. "Matthew." In *The Expositor's Bible Commentary.* Vol. 8: *Matthew, Mark, Luke,* edited by Frank E. Gaebelein. Grand Rapids: Zondervan, 1984.

Chan, Simon. *Liturgical Theology: The Church as Worshiping Community.* Downers Grove, IL: IVP Academic, 2006.

Craddock, Fred B. *Luke.* Interpretation. Louisville: John Knox, 1990.

Diderot, Denis. *Political Writings.* Translated and edited by John Hope Mason and Robert Wokler. Cambridge: Cambridge University Press, 1992.

Ebel, Eva. *Die Attraktivität früher christlicher Gemeinden: Die Gemeinde von Korinth im Spiegel griechisch-römischer Vereine.* WUNT 2/178. Tübingen: Mohr Siebeck, 2004.

Edwards, Jonathan. *A Treatise Concerning Religious Affections: In Three Parts.* Oak Harbor: Logos Research Systems, 1996.

Erastus, Thomas. *Gründtlicher bericht, wie die wort Christi Das ist mein leib etc. zuuerstehen seien.* Heidelberg: Lück, 1562.

Etzelmüller, Gregor, and Heike Springhart, eds. *Gottes Geist und menschlicher Geist.* Leipzig: Evangelische Verlangsanstalt, 2013.

Faust, Eberhard. *Pax Christi et Pax Caesaris: Religionsgeschichtliche, traditionsgeschichtliche und sozialgeschichtliche Studien zum Ephesebrief.* NTOA 24. Göttingen: Vandenhoeck & Ruprecht, 1993.

Forsyth, P. T. *Positive Preaching and the Modern Mind.* Carlisle, UK: Paternoster, 1998.

Frame, John M. *Salvation Belongs to the Lord: An Introduction to Systematic Theology.* Phillipsburg, NJ: P&R, 2006.

————. *A Theology of Lordship.* Vol. 4, *The Doctrine of the Word of God.* Phillipsburg, NJ: P&R, 2010.

Fretheim, Terence E. *Exodus.* Interpretation. Louisville: John Knox, 1991.

Gaebelein, Frank E., ed. *The Expositor's Bible Commentary.* Vol. 8: *Matthew, Mark, Luke.* Grand Rapids: Zondervan, 1984.

Gaffin, Richard. *Perspectives on Pentecost: Studies in New Testament Reading on the Gifts of the Holy Spirit.* Phillipsburg, NJ: P&R, 1979.

Gerhard, Johann. *Loci theologici.* 1st ed. 1610–1622.

Getz, Gene A. *Elders and Leaders: God's Plan for Leading the Church.* Chicago: Moody, 2003.

Godzik, Peter, ed. *Sterbebegleitung—herzlich und zugewandt.* Rosengarten bei Hamburg: Steinmann, 2012.

Gurnall, William. *The Christian in Complete Armour.* London: Tegg, 1845.

Hagner, Donald A. *Matthew 1–13.* WBC 33A. Dallas: Word, 2002.

Hare, Douglas R. A. *Matthew.* Interpretation. Louisville: John Knox, 1993.

Hauerwas, Stanley. *The Hauerwas Reader.* Edited by John Berkman and Michael Cartwright. Durham: Duke University Press, 2001.

Healy, Nicholas M. *Church, World and the Christian Life: Practical-Prophetic Ecclesiology.* Cambridge: Cambridge University Press, 2000.

Henry, Matthew. *Commentary on the Whole Bible: Complete and Unabridged in One Volume.* New modern ed. Peabody, MA: Hendrickson, 1991.

Herbst, Michael. "Minderheit mit Zukunft—Kirche zwischen Resignation und Aufbruch." *KuD* 51 (2005) 2–16.

Hodge, Charles. *Systematic Theology.* Vol. 1. Oak Harbor: Logos Research Systems, 1997.

———. *Systematic Theology.* Vol. 3. Grand Rapids: Eerdmans, 1946.

Huber, Wolfgang. "Volkskirche: Systematisch-theologisch." In *TRE* 35. Berlin: de Gruyter, 2003.

Hume, David. "Of the Standard of Taste." In *Essays Moral and Political.* London: Routledge, 1894.

James, William. *The Varieties of Religious Experience: A Study in Human Nature, Being the Gifford Lectures on Natural Religion Delivered at Edinburgh in 1901–1902.* Garden City, NY: Doubleday, 1978.

Jerome, St. *Commentary on Matthew 16:19.* Translated by Thomas P. Scheck. FC 117. Washington, DC: Catholic University of America, 2008.

Jobes, Karen H. *1 Peter.* BECNT. Grand Rapids: Baker Academic, 2005.

Kant, Immanuel. *Critique of Judgement.* Translated by J. H. Bernard. New York: Macmillan, 1951.

Kasper, Walter, ed. *Lexikon für Theologie und Kirche.* Vol. 9. 3rd ed. Freiburg: Herder, 2000.

Kertelge, Karl, ed. *Paulus in den neutestamentlichen Spätschriften: Zur Paulusrezeption im Neuen Testament.* QD 89. Freiburg: Herder, 1981.

Koyzis, David T. *Political Visions and Illusions: A Survey and Christian Critique of Contemporary Ideologies.* Downers Grove: IVP Academic, 2003.

Kristanto, Billy. "The Bible and Our Postmodern World." *ERT* 37 (2013) 153–65.

———. *Human Being - Being Human: A Theological Anthropology in Biblical, Historical, and Ecumenical Perspective.* International Theology 20. Berlin: Lang, 2020.

———. *The Place of Music in the Church and in Society.* Ethos Institute Engagement Series. Singapore: Ethos Institute for Public Christianity, 2018.

Leith, John H. "Calvin's Doctrine of the Proclamation of the Word and Its Significance for Today in the Light of Recent Research." *Review and Expositor* 86 (1989) 29–44.

Lévinas, Emmanuel. *Difficile liberté: Essais sur le judaïsme.* Paris: Michel, 1963, 2d ed. 1967, 1974.

———. *Entre Nous.* Translated by M. B. Smith and B. Harshav. New York: Columbia, 1998.

———. *Totality and Infinity: An Essay on Exteriority.* Translated by Alphonso Lingis. Pittsburgh: Duquesne University Press, 1969.

Lincoln, Andrew T. *Ephesians.* WBC 42. Dallas: Word, 2002.

Lindberg, Carter. *The European Reformations.* 2nd ed. Chichester, UK: Wiley-Blackwell, 2010.

Lloyd-Jones, D. Martyn, ed. *Puritan Papers*. Vol. 1: *1956–1959*. Phillipsburg, NJ: P&R, 2000.

Lossky, Vladimir. *The Mystical Theology of the Eastern Church*. London: James Clarke, 1957.

Luther, Martin. *Luther's Works*. Vol. 40. Edited by Jaroslav Pelikan et al. Philadelphia: Fortress, 1999.

———. *Luther's Works*. Vol. 47. Edited by Jaroslav Pelikan et al. Philadelphia: Fortress, 1999.

———. *Resolutiones Lutherianae super propositionibus suis Lipsiae disputatis*, 1519. In WA 2.

Maag, Karin. *Lifting Hearts to the Lord: Worship with John Calvin in Sixteenth-Century Geneva*. Grand Rapids: Eerdmans, 2016.

MacDougall, Scott. *More than Communion: Imagining an Eschatological Ecclesiology*. Ecclesiological Investigations 20. London: Bloomsbury T. & T. Clark, 2015.

Maxwell, William D. *An Outline of Christian Worship: Its Development and Forms*. London: Oxford University Press, 1963.

McClean, John. "Neo-Calvinism versus Two-Kingdoms: an eschatological assessment." *Reformed Theological Review* 76 (2017) 172–95.

McKee, Elsie Anne. *John Calvin and the Diaconate and Liturgical Almsgiving*. Geneva: Droz, 1984.

MacPherson, John. *Christian Dogmatics*. Edinburgh: T. & T. Clark, 1898.

Melanchthon, Philip. *Loci theologici* (1521). CR 21. New York: Johnson, 1963.

Meyer, Harding. "'Einheit in versöhnter Verschiedenheit': Eine ökumenische Zielvorstellung. Ihre Absicht, Entstehung und Bedeutung." *KuD* 61 (2015) 293–306.

Milbank, John. *Being Reconciled: Ontology and Pardon*. Radical Orthodoxy Series. London: Routledge, 2003.

———. *The Word Made Strange: Theology, Language, Culture*. Oxford: Blackwell, 1997.

Minear, Paul S. *Images of the Church in the New Testament*. Philadelphia: Westminster, 1960.

Möller, Christian. *Seelsorglich predigen: Die parakletische Dimension von Predigt, Seelsorge und Gemeinde*. 2nd ed. Göttingen: Vandenhoeck & Ruprecht, 1990.

Moo, Douglas J. *The Letters to the Colossians and to Philemon*. Grand Rapids: Eerdmans, 2008.

Mounce, William D. *Pastoral Epistles*. WBC 46. Nashville: Nelson, 2000.

Nash, Ronald H. "Shepherding Overseers." *Reformed Journal* 30/9 (1980) 3–4.

Nehamas, Alexander. *On Friendship*. New York: Basic, 2016.

———. *Only a Promise of Happiness: The Place of Beauty in a World of Art*. Princeton: Princeton University Press, 2007.

Niesel, Wilhelm. *Bekenntnisschriften und Kirchenordnungen: Der nach Gottes Wort reformierten Kirche*. Zürich: Zollikon, 1938.

Osborne, Grant R. *Revelation*. BECNT. Grand Rapids: Baker Academic, 2002.

Owen, John. *The Works of John Owen*. Vol. 4. Edited by W. H. Goold. Edinburgh: Banner of Truth, 1967.

———. *The Works of John Owen*. Vol. 11. Edited by W. H. Goold. Edinburgh: T. & T. Clark, 1862.

Parker, T. H. L. *Calvin's Preaching*. Louisville: Westminster John Knox, 1992.

Pictet, Benedict. *Christian Theology*. Translated by F. Reyroux. London: Seeley & Burnside, 1834.

Poole, Matthew. *Annotations upon the Holy Bible*. Vol. 3. New York: Carter, 1853.

BIBLIOGRAPHY

Puzynin, Andrey P. "Lord Radstock and the St. Petersburg Revival." *ERT* 37 (2013) 100–117.

Ramsey, A. M. *The Gospel and the Catholic Church.* London: Longmans, Green, 1936.

Rawls, J. *Justice as Fairness: A Restatement.* Edited by E. Kelly. Cambridge: Harvard University Press, 2001.

Ricoeur, Paul. *The Rule of Metaphor: Multi-Disciplinary Studies in the Creation of Meaning in Language.* Translated by Robert Czerny with Kathleen McLaughlin and John Costello, SJ. London: Routledge & Kegan Paul, 1986.

Ridderbos, H. N. *Paul: An Outline of His Theology.* Translated by J. R. De Witt. Grand Rapids: Eerdmans, 1975.

Rutherford, Samuel. *Due Right of Presbyteries, or, A Peaceable Plea for the Government of the Church of Scotland, Wherein Is Examined 1. The way of the Church of Christ in New England, in brotherly equality, and independency, or coordination, without subjection of one church to another. 2. Their apology for the said government, their answers to thirty and two questions are considered. 3. A treatise for a church covenant is discussed. 4. The arguments of Mr. Robinson in his justification of separation are discovered. 5. His treatise, called, The peoples plea for the exercise of prophecy, is tryed. 6. Diverse late arguments against presbyteriall government, and the power of synods are discussed, the power of the prince in matters ecclesiastical modestly considered, & divers incident controversies resolved.* London: E. Griffin for Richard Whittaker and Andrew Crook, 1644.

Ryle, J. C. *Holiness: Its Nature, Hindrances, Difficulties and Roots.* London: Hunt, 1889.

Schaff, P., and H. Wace, eds. *NPNF* II/14. New York: Scribner, 1900.

Schlink, Edmund. *Schriften zu Ökumene und Bekenntnis.* Vol. 1, *Der kommende Christus und die kirchlichen Traditionen. Nach dem Konzil.* Göttingen: Vandenhoeck & Ruprecht, 2004.

———. *Schriften zu Ökumene und Bekenntnis.* Vol. 2: *Ökumenische Dogmatik.* Göttingen: Vandenhoeck & Ruprecht, 2005.

Schmid, Heinrich. *The Doctrinal Theology of the Evangelical Lutheran Church, Verified from the Original Sources.* Translated by C. A. Hay and H. E. Jacobs. 2nd English ed., rev. acc. to the 6th German ed. Philadelphia: Lutheran Publication Society, 1889.

Schnelle, Udo. *Apostle Paul: His Life and Theology.* Translated by M. Eugene Boring. Grand Rapids: Baker Academic, 2005.

———. *Einleitung in das Neue Testament.* 5th ed. Göttingen: Vandenhoeck & Ruprecht, 2005. ET = *History and Theology of the New Testament Writings.* Translated by M. Eugene Boring. Minneapolis: Fortress, 1998.

———. *Theology of the New Testament.* Translated by M. Eugene Boring. Grand Rapids: Baker Academic, 2009.

Schwier, H., ed. *Geöffnet: Raum und Wort in der Heidelberger Universitätskirche.* Frankfurt: Lembeck, 2006.

Scruton, Roger. *Beauty.* Oxford: Oxford University Press, 2009.

Smith, James K. A. *Desiring the Kingdom: Worship, Worldview, and Cultural Formation.* Grand Rapids: Baker Academic, 2009.

Smith, James K. A., and James H. Olthuis, eds. *Radical Orthodoxy and the Reformed Tradition.* Grand Rapids: Baker Academic, 2005.

Stackhouse, Max L., ed. *God and Globalization.* Vol. 2, *The Spirit and the Modern Authorities.* Harrisburg, PA: Trinity, 2001.

———. *God and Globalization.* Vol. 4, *Globalization and Grace.* New York: Continuum, 2007.

————. *Public Theology and Political Economy: Christian Stewardship in Modern Society.* Grand Rapids: Eerdmans, 1987.

Stott, John R. W. *The Message of the Sermon on the Mount (Matthew 5–7): Christian Counter-Culture.* Leicester, UK: InterVarsity, 1985.

————. *What Christ Thinks of the Church.* Grand Rapids: Eerdmans, 1958.

Stout, Tracey Mark. "Church, World and the Christian Life: Practical Prophetic Ecclesiology." *Journal of Church and State* 43 (2001) 345–46.

Strohm, Christoph. "Calvin and Religious Tolerance." In *John Calvin's Impact on Church and Society, 1509–2009,* edited by M. E. Hirzel and M. Sallmann, 175–91. Grand Rapids: Eerdmans, 2009.

Thiselton, Anthony C. *The First Epistle to the Corinthians: A Commentary on the Greek Text.* Grand Rapids: Eerdmans, 2000.

Tjørhom, Ola. "Better Together: Apostolicity and Apostolic Succession in Light of An Ecumenical Ecclesiology." *Pro Ecclesia* 23 (2014) 282–93.

Tuininga, Matthew J. "Good News for the Poor: An Analysis of Calvin's Concept of Poor Relief and the Diaconate in Light of His Two Kingdoms Paradigm." *CTJ* 49 (2014) 221–47.

Van der Kooi, Cornelis, and Gijsbert Van den Brink. *Christian Dogmatics: An Introduction.* Translated by Reinder Bruinsma with James D. Bratt. Grand Rapids: Eerdmans, 2017.

Vanhoozer, Kevin J., ed. *Dictionary for Theological Interpretation of the Bible.* Grand Rapids: Baker Academic, 2005.

Venema, Cornelis P. "Sacraments and Baptism in the Reformed Confessions." *MTJ* 11 (2000) 21–86.

Volf, Miroslav et al., eds. *The Future of Theology: Essays in Honor of Jürgen Moltmann.* Grand Rapids: Eerdmans, 1996.

Wagner, E. Glenn. *Escape from Church, Inc.: The Return of the Pastor-Shepherd.* Grand Rapids: Zondervan, 2011.

Wainright, Geoffrey. *Doxology: The Praise of God in Worship, Doctrine, and Life.* New York: Oxford University Press, 1980.

Webster, John. "On Evangelical Ecclesiology." In *Confessing God: Essays in Christian Dogmatics II.* London: Bloomsbury T. & T. Clark, 2005.

————. *Word and Church: Essays in Christian Dogmatics.* Edinburgh: T. & T. Clark, 2001.

Welker, Michael. *God the Revealed: Christology.* Grand Rapids: Eerdmans, 2013.

————. "Kirche und Diakonie in säkularen Kontexten." *ZevKr* 60 (2015) 27–40.

————. "Die Reformation als geistliche Erneuerung und bleibende Aufgabe in Theologien und Kirchen." *Evangelische Theologie* 73 (2013) 166–177.

————. "Serving God in a Time When a World-view Collapses: The Pastor-Theologian at the Beginning of the Third Millennium." In *Loving God with Our Minds: The Pastor as Theologian,* edited by Michael Welker and Cynthia A. Jarvis, 74–88. Grand Rapids: Eerdmans, 2004.

Welker, Michael, and David Willis, eds. *Toward the Future of Reformed Theology: Tasks, Topics, Traditions.* Grand Rapids: Eerdmans, 1999.

————. *What Happens in Holy Communion?* Grand Rapids: Eerdmans, 2000.

Wenham, Gordon J. *Genesis 1–15.* WBC 1. Dallas: Word, 2002.

Zwingli, Huldreich. *The Latin Works of Huldreich Zwingli.* Vol. 2. Edited by W. J. Hinke. Philadelphia: Heidelberg, 1922.

————. *The Latin Works of Huldreich Zwingli.* Vol. 3. Edited by C. N. Heller. Philadelphia: Heidelberg, 1929.

Name/Subject Index